Partnering
for
Performance

Partnering
for
Performance

Unleashing the Power of Finance in the 21st-Century Organization

Martin G. Mand
William Whipple III

AMACOM
American Management Association

New York • Atlanta • Boston • Chicago • Kansas City • San Francisco • Washington, D. C.
Brussels • Mexico City • Tokyo • Toronto

Special discounts on bulk quantities of AMACOM books are available to corporations, professional associations, and other organizations. For details, contact Special Sales Department, AMACOM, a division of American Management Association,
1601 Broadway, New York, NY 10019.
Tel.: 212-903-8316 Fax: 212-903-8083
Web site: www.amanet.org

This publication is designed to provide accurate and authoritative information in regard to the subject matter covered. It is sold with the understanding that the publisher is not engaged in rendering legal, accounting, or other professional service. If legal advice or other expert assistance is required, the services of a competent professional person should be sought.

Library of Congress Cataloging-in-Publication Data

Mand, Martin G.
Partnering for performance : unleashing the power of finance in the 21st-century organization /
Martin G. Mand and William Whipple III.
    p.   cm.
    Includes bibliographical references and index.
    ISBN 0-8144-0556-8
    1. Business enterprises—Finance.   I. Title.
HG1026.M354   2000
658.15—dc21   *00-029964*

Printing number
10   9   8   7   6   5   4   3   2   1

CONTENTS

PREFACE

This book was written with the intent of helping organizations improve their performance in a very competitive and fast changing economic environment. It reflects our beliefs that Finance has often been underutilized as an organizational asset and resource, and that a *Partnering for Performance* (PFP) strategy between the operating people and Finance can contribute immensely to organizational success and the creation of shareholder value.

Our book begins with the profound changes that are transforming the business and financial world. It then turns to the collective thinking, practices, and behaviors (or new mindset) required by Finance people and others they will work with in the organization to turn PFP into a reality. We believe PFP is essential for the new forms and structures of organizations (e.g., more horizontal than vertical; more delegation and fewer people; a pronounced blurring of organizational boundaries; virtual organizations) that are being created to address the opportunities and challenges of the 21st century. The new mindset is also essential if Finance is to realize its true potential by becoming *Shareholder Value Enablers* (SVE).

Consistent with our business experience, the primary focus is on the financial issues that arise in a large company. The issues discussed also apply to smaller businesses, and many apply to nonprofit organizations and governmental agencies. We have attempted to represent all types of organizations in the discussion.

You should be aware that this is not a Finance "how-to"

book about the tools of the trade. Neither is it about financial reengineering (i.e., cost reduction), which is only a road to efficiency, or even about reinventing Finance (i.e., redesigning systems and realigning responsibilities) so as to increase effectiveness. Nor is it a textbook, an academic discussion, or a research study.

Instead, this book is the thoughts of two practitioners with more than fifty years of combined knowledge and observations of Finance's role in organizations. It is intended to express a new and emerging view of Finance and its role in competitive strategy, capital effectiveness, and increasing shareholder value, and it explains how this new role can be implemented through PFP. We have striven to keep the language as plain as possible. Over sixty real-world examples demonstrate that the ideas presented are not theory, but practical applications.

We have written the book in an easy-to-read style to facilitate understanding of the material by people with limited available reading time. Our Tips for Readers may also be helpful.

As a framework for the book, the reader listens in on a continuing dialogue between the chief executive officer and the chief financial officer of an imaginary company, who are discussing the benefits that can be achieved by implementing a new and different role for Finance. This device provides a convenient way to challenge viewpoints and demonstrate that wisdom exists on both sides of the decision-making table. It is also appropriate since the joint efforts of CEOs and CFOs will be required to implement the shareholder value creating messages of this book for the benefit of all their stakeholders (shareholders, employees, customers, suppliers, and communities).

For those who will help to make the PFP and SVE vision a reality, we are confident that participation in this undertaking can only benefit your personal careers. Many people should find this book of interest, including:

> current organizational leaders and those who aspire to future leadership positions, including the CEOs and CFOs of the 21st century

➤ operating and Finance people who work together to achieve organizational and personal objectives

➤ entrepreneurs who are seeking to grow small businesses into large successful ones

➤ students and professors of business and finance courses who desire to understand the practical, as well as theoretical, aspects of these subjects

➤ consultants who advise organizations on ways to achieve improved performance

➤ bankers, accountants, and others who have an interest in Finance and the management of organizations

➤ leaders and employees of government and non-profit agencies

➤ anyone with an interest in where prosperity comes from and the future welfare of the global village

We hope that after reading this book you will use our strategies, experiences, and observations to add value to your own organization and to your personal life. If so, we will have accomplished our purpose.

TIPS FOR READERS

Recognizing that you are very busy people with varying interests and learning objectives, here are some suggestions as to how this book might be read:

➤ *"What I want are the key insights."* The Summing Up sections at the end of each chapter cover the most important conclusions of the book. See also Chapter Ten for an overall recap in a lighter vein.

➤ *"Never mind the answers, I'm interested in the reasoning."* The ongoing dialogue between the CEO and the CFO provides an outline of the text, starting with the challenges that organizations face in attracting funding in today's financial world (Chapters One and Two) and continuing through evaluating the implementation of PFP (Chapter Nine). If a particular issue catches your interest, read the following text for a more extended discussion.

➤ *"Been there, done that, but I'm interested in the experiences of other organizations."* Browsing through the book, you will find over sixty real-world examples that have been included to illustrate points in the discussion..

➤ *"I need the answer to a particular question."* This is not a technical or "how-to" book, but there are specifics on various concepts and techniques, such as the cost of capital, discounted cash flow measures, budgeting, decision and risk analysis, options, compensation, and incentives. Scan the Contents and the Index to see if there is discussion relevant to your query.

➤ *"We know what to do, but need some diagnostic tools."* Chapter Nine provides several checklists and an organizational troubleshooting guide. They were not designed for any particular organization, of course, but may provide you with a useful starting point for designing your own diagnostic tools.

➤ *"I need to understand how Finance can become a source of competitive advantage. for our organization, from soup to nuts."* Our advice is to read the whole book, and we sincerely hope that you will enjoy it.

ACKNOWLEDGMENTS

We wish to express our gratitude to Frederick C. Militello, Jr., president and chief executive officer of Finquest Partners, Inc., Cornwallville, New York, and one of the intended coauthors of this book. Fred made a major contribution by developing many of the themes and ideas expressed herein when he participated in the preparation of an outline for the book. Unfortunately, because of his business and personal commitments, he did not have the time to participate in the writing of the manuscript.

We also wish to thank three reviewers who volunteered to read a draft of the book and gave us many ideas and suggestions for improvement. They are:

➤ William G. Shenkir, William Stamps Farish professor of Free Enterprise, and former dean of the McIntire School of Commerce of the University of Virginia, Charlottesville, Virginia

➤ Michael E. Mand, a son of Martin G. Mand, a public relations executive, and a writer based in Los Angeles, California

➤ William Whipple Jr., the father of William Whipple III, a retired brigadier general in the U.S. Army Corps of Engineers, and a water resources consultant who resides in Princeton, New Jersey

Thanks are due as well to our editors at AMACOM—Ray O'Connell, senior acquisitions and planning editor, who provided vital help and encouragement throughout this project and

Shelly Wert, associate editor, who guided us through the production process.

It is only fitting to also mention the many people that we have respectively shared ideas with about financial and business issues over the years, especially former colleagues at DuPont and Northern Telecom. Their perspectives and views contributed to our understanding of the subject matter in ways too numerous to enumerate.

Lastly, our thanks go to our wives, Shelly Mand and Valerie Whipple, who encouraged us to undertake the challenge of writing a book for the benefit of those who would follow us in the business world; and to our children, Gregory, Michael, and Brian Mand; and Julie Jefferson, Lara, and Jennifer Whipple, who are always an inspiration to us.

Marty Mand and Bill Whipple

INTRODUCTION

Say that you are the chief executive officer of a public company. It could be an S&P 500 company, an old-line manufacturer from the Midwest, or an Internet startup.

Having been around the block a couple of times, you are familiar with the major models for driving business excellence. All of them have merits, you have concluded, but not one of them is a panacea.

Marketing focus is critical, and any company that loses it will not last very long. An excessive emphasis on meeting customer needs in the here and now, however, can obscure the possibility of offering something that present or potential customers have never thought of and do not realize they want. Products or services that consistently exceed expectations can be expensive, creating opportunities for competitors to offer lower-priced products or services.

Put the company's money into research, and build a better mousetrap? Great idea, but research and development costs big bucks, and the competition is doing it too. Besides, originators of major technological breakthroughs are not always the ones who succeed in exploiting them commercially.

Improving all business processes to lower costs seems like a no-brainer. Mistakes are costly, and they can be reduced dramatically by closer attention to process steps. Hit enough singles, to use a baseball analogy, and you will not need to worry about swinging for the fences. On the other hand, too much stress on doing everything right the first time can foster a zero defects mentality that is antithetical to innovation and creativity.

Paying attention to the corporate culture can be of great benefit, because employees with a sense of fitting in will tend to work harder and more effectively. Again the law of diminishing returns must be considered, however, for at some point excessive concern about individual sensibilities will begin to undermine business focus.

You are reflecting on these things now because the quarterly earnings were disappointing, and this time the stock price took a hit. The board is going to want to hear what you propose to do about the situation, and you have been stewing about what to tell them for several days.

The worst part of it is that you do not have any clear-cut sense of the answer. There are many things to work on, as always, but none of the issues on your hit list promises to make a huge difference. It might be time to schedule another offsite meeting or call in a management consultant, but you cannot summon up much enthusiasm for either option.

In your stack of phone messages, there is a note that the chief financial officer called about "shareholder value enabling." Must be a pitch for something, probably a new financial performance measure or another round of belt-tightening—elimination of a couple of slow moving products, a moratorium on nonessential travel, a hiring freeze, or whatever.

It would be nice, you think, while jotting a note for your administrative assistant to schedule a meeting with the CFO, if Finance could come up with something more creative for a change to show they had a real handle on the business situation.

Partnering
for
Performance

▌ *Chapter One* ▌

TODAY'S BUSINESS AND FINANCIAL WORLD

All is flux, nothing stays still.

Heraclitus, circa 500 B.C.

CEO: Glad we could get together; it doesn't happen very often except at staff meetings. Well, I suppose you would like to talk about
the earnings shortfall.
CFO: Actually, I was hoping we could discuss some other things,
starting with the triumph of capitalism and financial markets, and
then get into the enhanced role that Finance could play in helping
the company achieve its objectives.

Despite rapid economic growth, the world's resources are
dwarfed by the sum of human needs and desires. Consider that
the global population has increased by two billion people in the
past twenty-five years, which is more people than were alive in
1900. For those who might find this rapid growth alarming, it
may be of some comfort that the year 2000 population is about
five hundred million less than demographic experts were pro-
jecting in the 1970s.

Individual aspirations have grown far faster than the population, driven by (a) technological progress that makes many

things possible that could formerly only be imagined, and (b) readily available information about the lifestyle of the more prosperous members of the "global village" that others hope to emulate.

Until the day comes when everyone is a millionaire, society's resources must be allocated—through one mechanism or another—to whatever are deemed to be the most important uses. Thus, society must choose:

➤ what goods and services will be produced, in what amounts, and for whom
➤ how much of the current output will be currently consumed, and how much will be allocated to productive investment to keep the economic pie growing
➤ which of the many possible investment proposals will be undertaken

Government ownership and operation of the economy offers a possible answer to the allocation issue, but one that has been thoroughly discredited. Socialism never did work very well, and the accelerating pace of technological change (creating ever more choices to be managed) has undermined this model. Witness the collapse of the Soviet Union, the proliferation of free market mechanisms in China, and the decisions of many other countries to sell off economic enterprises that were formerly government-owned and make them subject to private sector competition. For instance, state-owned telephone companies have been privatized in one country after another, clearing the way for transnational combinations and a global telecommunications market.

Some governments have also lifted regulatory restrictions in many industries, e.g., airlines, telecommunications, and power generation. A notable recent example is the repeal of the U.S. Glass-Steagall Act, which was enacted in the 1930s, to mandate a separation of banking, investment banking, and insurance operations. The Glass-Steagall restrictions were already subject to many exceptions, but now the way had officially been cleared for the creation of true financial service supermarkets.

Hybrid approaches to resource allocation (e.g., centralized government planning with private execution) are also out of favor. It has been a while since anyone wrote with conviction about the Japanese economic miracle, although it is surely possible that Japan will adjust its approach and come back stronger than ever.

Even the status of national entities has been challenged, with the tendency being to create regional associations for economic purposes while allowing increasing local autonomy in other areas. This is essentially a form of federalism, a political structure that by and large has served the United States very well over the years.

> Example: Having begun with the elimination of trade barriers, a process that has been emulated by other regional trade blocs such as NAFTA and LAFTA, the European Union (EU) has been working to harmonize other economic and social policies. Moreover, eleven member countries (the UK, Sweden, Denmark, and Greece will probably fall in line eventually) are launching the euro to replace their individual currencies.
>
> The emergence of the euro will eliminate currency risk and exchange cost for investors within the euro-zone, and the volume of EU bond issues has already soared. There has also been a surge in European merger and acquisition activity, with over one trillion dollars worth of deals in the first half of 1999.
>
> In the years ahead, the European economy seems destined to undergo a true renaissance. Small wonder that almost every country in Eastern Europe plus Turkey has applied for EU membership.[1]

If only by default, capitalism has emerged as the world's prime economic model. The premise of capitalism is that economic choices are best made by free market mechanisms. Instead of the government deciding how many cars, trucks, SUVs, and so on, should be built, consumers can decide which vehicles they want to buy at the prices at which competing producers offer them for sale.

Furthermore, consumers can decide whether they want to buy new vehicles at all or spend their money instead on the myriad of other products and services that are available. In recent years, service and computer-related businesses have grown rapidly, while many conventional manufacturing businesses languished. No wonder the central planners found it difficult to manage national economies.

CEO: According to what I read, capitalism and free market mechanisms are still often challenged.

CFO: Very true, which just goes to show there are no final answers in life.

For all their efficiency, free markets do not necessarily ensure the equitable distribution of resources or address social issues (such as environmental effects or child labor) that fall outside the revenue and cost equation. For instance, one could raise legitimate questions as to the wisdom of producing all those millions of vans, trucks, and SUVs, when most of the buyers could get around without major inconvenience in more fuel-efficient, lower emission automobiles.

Although capitalism seems to have triumphed, social constraints will still compete with capitalism. In the United States, at least, people with a grievance are conditioned to consult an attorney or demand government intervention at the drop of a hat. Any company that fails to keep the public reasonably satisfied can expect such action.

Example: During a snowstorm that blanketed the Chicago area in early 1999, Northwest Airlines made a bad call and failed to divert arriving flights. Thousands of passengers were confined for hours in planes parked on the tarmac, and bitterly complained about the experience afterwards. This led to much discussion in Congress about the need to "fix" a mistake that was unlikely to recur, which quickly led to a general review of industry practices.

The major airlines responded in September 1999 with a twelve-point "Customers First" commitment to provide timely notification of travel delays, meet the essential needs of passengers trapped on the ground for lengthy periods, respond promptly to customer complaints, increase luggage-liability limits, etc. Some critics characterized the industry response as inadequate, and continued to support mandatory legislation.

In some instances, it seems (to businesspeople at least) that efforts to enforce social responsibility are carried to extremes. A business can face staggering penalties in a court of law, whether or not it was primarily to blame for the plaintiff's injuries.

Example: In a recent case, a 1979 Chevrolet Malibu that had been purchased used for $500 was rammed by a drunk driver travelling at a high rate of speed. The occupants of the first vehicle sued General Motors, blaming their severe injuries on an alleged decision two decades earlier to sacrifice safety for profits. The most dramatic supporting evidence was a memo written in 1973 by a 22-year-old GM engineer and the notes of an attorney who interviewed him in 1981. GM was allegedly prevented from presenting evidence that the design the plaintiff's attorneys suggested should have been built was no safer than the design actually chosen.

The jury awarded $4.9 billion in compensatory and punitive damages to the plaintiffs, an amount exceeding all of GM's earnings (reflecting the efforts of many thousands of employees) for the preceding year. The trial judge reduced the verdict to a still staggering $1.2 billion, and this result was appealed.

New technology also faces challenges, such as the European backlash against genetically altered crops (labeled "Frankenfood" in some quarters). At stake are billions of dollars in U.S.

agricultural exports, and the prospects of biotechnology companies seeking to dramatically increase plant yields, enhance the nutritional value of crops, and reduce the need for agricultural chemicals (which also involve environmental risks).

The opposition to genetically modified organisms wants marketing of altered crops to be postponed until it is demonstrated that they pose no conceivable risks. Such a demonstration would be impossible, of course, just as European wine and unpasteurized cheese exported to the United States cannot be absolutely guaranteed.

CEO: Obviously, the business world is going global. What do you consider to be the major drivers for this development, and what do you see as the implications?

CFO: Globalization is the inevitable result of technological development. It will benefit the strongest competitors and put the laggards at risk.

Although it has been around so long that there is a tendency to take it for granted, fast, reliable, and relatively economical air transportation has dramatically shrunk the globe. Once a week or so was required to cross the Atlantic by ship; now one can go almost anywhere in a fraction of the time.

Similarly, telephone service has become increasingly reliable and economical, faxes have replaced telexes for document transmission, and videoconferencing is becoming more common. Consequently, many communication needs can be met without taking a trip at all.

Then there is the networking of company computers (Intranet) and of all computers (Internet), making it possible to zap information to multiple users around the globe at virtually zero cost. There are no more worries about time zones; e-mails can be sent and read at the sender's or recipient's convenience.

Information does not even have to be sent any more. Just post it on the computer system, and authorized users everywhere can access the information when they need it. If the information needs to be changed or updated, the sender can provide users with instant access to the new version without incurring the expense of mailing out revised copies.

Communications aside, the advances in information technology have had an enormous impact on business operations. Consider the ease of accessing data stored on internal computer systems (data warehousing), the ability to obtain and organize data from external sources (data mining), the effortless and rapid performance of repetitive calculations, and so on.

Significant benefits have also been realized through the use of shared computer systems. For instance, American Airlines made the SABRE airline reservation system available to travel agents, thereby gaining a significant marketing advantage for its own flights. Another common application for manufacturers is to set up electronic data interchange (EDI) system links with suppliers as a means of facilitating "just-in-time" inventory management and paying bills more efficiently.

What lies ahead? In 1899, Charles Duell, director of the U.S. Patent Office, said that the office could be eliminated because "everything that can be invented has been invented." Instead, the 20th century has seen more technological breakthroughs than any other. There is every reason to believe that the rate of change will continue to be rapid.

New technology has dramatically affected the structure and functioning of economic enterprises. Multinational companies are hardly new, but traditionally they kept their core activities at home. The idea was to locate marketing groups and finishing plants in other countries just enough to establish a local presence. Now the mindset is to locate all of the firm's operations, including basic manufacturing facilities and research and development labs, wherever it makes the most sense from a global economic standpoint.

The manner in which dispersed operations work together can be just as important as their location. At Nortel Networks (formerly known as Northern Telecom), for instance, it is possible to work on a technical problem around the clock by passing work from a group in North America to a second group in Asia to be upgraded and then passed on to a third group in Europe.

By the time the people in North America come to work the next day, their previous work has been extended and refined, giving them a new base from which to start.

At one time, all the major mergers involved companies in the same country. Now there are also mergers of large companies with headquarters on different continents, e.g., British Petroleum and Amoco and Daimler-Benz and Chrysler. Such a shift should not be surprising, for at some point any company that truly aspires to become a global enterprise must shed its national identity. Kenichi Ohmae, a well-known writer on global strategic issues, says:

> *There is no single best way to avoid or overcome near-sightedness. An equidistant perspective can take many forms. However managers do it, however they get there, building a value system that emphasizes seeing and thinking globally is the bottom-line price of admission to today's borderless economy.*[2]

This is not to say that all successful businesses are global in scope, but even a small business, competing in a limited geographic area, is a part of the global economy. Go to any U.S. department store and check the source of the merchandise. In addition to products made in this country, there will be items from every corner of the globe. U.S. products similarly find their way into stores around the world, e.g., L. L. Bean sells many millions of dollars of merchandise in Japan.

Then there are all those components produced in one part of the world and assembled into products in another. An earthquake in Taiwan recently resulted in a shortage of memory chips, for instance, that temporarily disrupted the operations of several U.S. personal computer manufacturers.

Even if a business winds up going global, it has to start somewhere. McDonald's began as a hamburger stand in San Bernardino, California, in the 1950s. The concept caught on after salesman Ray Kroc got involved, first in the United States and then almost everywhere. Today, half of the company's revenues and most of its growth are outside the United States.

CEO: You haven't mentioned e-commerce yet. Many people say this emerging technology is so revolutionary that it will change the basic business model.

CFO: From a market perspective, e-commerce offers more choices to consumers everywhere. Goods and services will increasingly be purchased without regard to where they come from, based on price, quality, customer service, or any combination thereof.

The basis for e-commerce is the Internet, an unbeatably cheap way to make information available to interested parties and communicate with them about it. Such information is not limited to words and numbers, but can include lifelike color pictures, videos, and sound.

Instead of selling its products or services through stores, distributors, direct mail, telemarketing, or its door-to-door sales force, a business can now sell them online. A potential customer reviews the information that is posted, decides to make an offer or purchase, fills out the quote or order form including credit card information, and clicks the mouse. That's it, even if the parties to the transaction are halfway around the globe from each other.

In addition to the potential elimination of market intermediaries, e-commerce transactions are not currently subject to sales and use taxes. But watch out, because ultimately a growing sector of the economy cannot be exempted from taxes without unfairly penalizing traditional businesses.

CEO: So everything will be sold on the Internet and the shopping malls will go bankrupt?

CFO: My fearless prediction is no, and not just because of the allure of what has been disdainfully referred to as "recreational shopping."

Many people want to examine products, try out merchandise, and ask questions before they make a purchase. They also want a place to return items that are not satisfactory. Even if such people get used to surfing the net for the lowest price, or having a search engine (a.k.a. shopping robot or "shopbot") do it for them, they will probably continue to make their purchases at physical stores.

Moreover, a solid physical presence (or "bricks and mortar") can contribute importantly to the success of an e-commerce venture. Visitors to the Nordstrom Web site, for instance, may be attracted initially by their familiarity with the company's upscale department stores.

On the other hand, buying products online appeals to people who are pressed for time and would like the convenience of shopping from home at whatever time happens to suit them. This will be particularly true if some of the cost savings inherent in e-commerce are used to support promotional offers (e.g., bonus frequent flyer miles for ordering airline tickets online) or reflected in lower selling prices.

Exploitation of the Internet is just getting started, and it is hard to predict how things will develop. The potential of e-commerce clearly extends beyond incidental transactions, such as bidding for collectable items at electronic auctions, to traditional "big ticket" purchases and transactions between businesses.

Example: It was recently announced that Ford will take a significant minority interest in Microsoft's car-buying Web site, thereby gaining the capability to bypass dealers and communicate directly with customers. The key objective, which General Motors and Toyota are pursuing with other partners, is to be able to manufacture cars meeting a customer's specifications (e.g., configuration, options, color) in days rather than weeks.

Implementation of online selling of automobiles is proceeding faster in countries outside the United States, because the car factories in the United States tend to be older, and the role of dealers is well established. In Taiwan, for instance, General Motors will be building cars to order very soon.

In addition to the marketing implications of e-commerce, the Internet has great potential for linking up manufacturers with their suppliers, greatly facilitating the exchange of information within a complex supply chain. The basic thrust is similar to the older EDI systems. Ford and General Motors are pursuing e-commerce initiatives to put their purchasing operations online, both in the United States and elsewhere.

The build-to-order concept has been in use for some time in the personal computer industry, including a seamless linkage to suppliers.

> Example: By taking orders through its Web site, Dell Computer can be sure of producing the models that customers want. As a result, slow moving models do not accumulate in inventory while fast moving models are sold out. Dell has also reduced distribution costs by selling its personal computers online rather than through stores.
>
> The information in Dell's order and production scheduling system is shared with suppliers, thereby enabling them to keep the necessary components—hard drives, motherboards, modems, etc.,—flowing to Dell's factories in the necessary quantities without a lot of back and forth communications. Dell's need for buffer inventories is minimized, thereby reducing working capital and potential inventory losses due to technological obsolescence.
>
> Other computer companies have established similar systems, but pioneer Dell gained significant market share and could soon pass Compaq and become the world's number one producer of personal computers.

E-commerce's potential to enhance competition will be manifested in many ways, including the blurring of the concept of geographic markets. It cannot be overemphasized that all businesses are part of the global economy. The challenge will be to turn this fact into an opportunity rather than a source of weakness.

Example: A mid-sized company in the Midwest used to have approximately 60 percent of the market in inexpensive dinnerware within a hundred-mile radius of its factory. Because such china is heavy and fragile, it has traditionally been sold within a small area. The company quickly lost more than half of its market after one of its customers, a hospital cafeteria, spotted a Web posting by a European manufacturer that offered equivalent (or better) china at a lower price and shipped it cheaply by air. Within a few months, many of the large china buyers in the area shifted to the European supplier.[3]

CEO: What other new technologies could affect the business world?
CFO: Some have predicted that the 21st century will be the Age of Biology. Space travel and advances in chaos theory could also be important.

The genetic codes for living organisms were *terra incognita* only a quarter century ago, but this is no longer true. As discussed earlier, genetically altered crops are already being cultivated commercially. Another harbinger of change is the smarter, longer-living mice that are now being created for experimental purposes. Imagine the potential consequences if some of those mice got loose.

The mapping of the typical human genetic code (or genome) will be complete within a few years, laying the foundation for some remarkable new possibilities. Parents who choose to do so will be able to determine the sex of their children before birth. It will be possible to correct genetic weaknesses that would otherwise result in lifelong disabilities or early death. Worn-out or defective body parts will be regenerated from stem cells instead of relying on the availability of replacements from compatible donors. New pharmaceutical products will be designed with increasing precision instead of being identified through empirical testing on laboratory animals. In sum, the average length and quality of human life can be expected to increase significantly.

Genetic modification is a controversial subject, and the social implications still need to be sorted out, but there is little doubt that this new technology will be used in one way or another. Companies in the pharmaceuticals, health care, and agricultural industries that find profitable ways to capitalize on the new technology will flourish, while their competitors fall by the wayside. Indirectly, the effects of genetic changes on demographics and consumer preferences will have a major impact on many industries.

Space is another frontier. Human explorers reached the moon in the 1960s. With the tremendous technological advances that have taken place since then, the colonization of Mars and other parts of the solar system can begin soon. Just think of the resulting business for aerospace companies and producers of high technology materials.

Advances in chaos theory will create the potential to model and understand complex, discontinuous phenomena, such as avalanches, earthquakes, and weather systems. Understanding why something happens is the first step to influencing it.

Imagine the implications of being able to control the weather, instead of (to paraphrase Mark Twain) simply talking about it. Beachfront real estate would boom, casualty insurance rates would drop, and the markets for umbrellas would be problematic (because of a likely consensus to allow rain to fall only at night).

Do some of these things sound fantastic? Sure, but people living in 1900 would have felt the same way about the Internet or people walking on the moon. The 21st century will be an exciting ride.

CEO: Fascinating—I had no idea you followed such developments. Still, something tells me you didn't come here to talk about future technology. What else is on your mind this afternoon?

CFO: I'd like to move on to how funds get allocated to productive investments via the financial markets, which could significantly affect this company's future prospects. The process may seem simple, but even at the individual level it's far from obvious what sort of choices will result. When all the millions of players are factored in, and governments overseeing the financial markets as well, the scope and complexity of the system becomes mind-boggling.

Here is a model of how the free market system allocates resources between consumption and investment:

1. Individuals make choices between spending in the here-and-now and saving for future needs (this year's vacation, a rainy day fund, retirement, and so on). Except to the extent that the government elects to intervene, e.g., by establishing a social safety net and collecting the taxes to pay for it, an evaluation of the tradeoffs involved is up to the individual. Who can say whether all those millions of people are making the right decisions, either individually or collectively?

Businesses do not choose between consumption and investment *per se*, but their decisions as to how much cash flow should be reinvested and how much should be paid out to owners are another important factor in the overall consumption and investment equation.

2. Rather than keeping their savings under a mattress, most people seek a return. There are many ways to do this, generally involving a financial intermediary. Funds can be deposited in an interest-bearing bank account, applied to credit card debt, used to buy life insurance, left in a 401K, invested through a broker in the stock market, and so on.

The available level of return will depend, among other things, on an investor's timeframe and risk tolerance. Longer-term investments with greater risk typically offer higher returns than shorter-term investments with relatively low risk.

Proposals surface periodically that seem to offer the best of both worlds, and even sophisticated investors can wind up getting burned, primarily as a result of their own wishful thinking. If a smooth-talking promoter with seemingly impeccable credentials "guarantees" a 50 percent return in six months, a smart thing to do is head for the nearest exit.

3. Funds diverted from current consumption are invested in debt obligations or equity securities. Either way, the ability of business firms to undertake productive investments is enhanced, providing fuel for economic growth.

On the other side of the equation, numerous organizations, from businesses, both large and small, to nonprofits and governments, are seeking money for the initiatives deemed necessary or desirable to support their respective objectives. The eligibility of businesses for funding will be assessed based on a combination of the financial return that is offered and the degree of assurance that it can be delivered. Nonbusiness organizations must demonstrate that they are adding value, i.e., that the value of their activities exceeds the cost.

The higher the perceived investment risk is, the higher is the return expected. Moreover, the global supply of capital is limited, and some organizations will be unable to attract the funding that they want.

Between investors and the organizations seeking funding are the financial markets, which match up the supply of and demand for investment funds around the globe. Financial markets are used here to mean commercial banks, investment banks, investment fund managers, investment analysts, securities brokers, and stock exchanges that together facilitate the investment process.

In theory, investors could cut out the intermediaries and lend money to or buy securities directly from the organizations concerned. In practice, there are too many people involved, and they do not know each other, particularly if the funds are being made available in one area and invested halfway around the globe. Also, the intermediaries provide a value-adding contribution by ensuring a competitive market and providing investors with information about investment alternatives.

If nothing else, investors will need help with some of the new derivative products that are being created. It is no longer simply a question of which company's stock to buy, but whether one wants to buy tracking stock, convertible preferred, PERCS, ACES, etc., or to buy "plain vanilla" equity issues.

This is not to say that the traditional role and compensation of financial intermediaries is sacrosanct. The commission income of brokers on the sale and purchase of securities is a good example. After the Securities and Exchange Commission (SEC) supported an end to fixed commissions on stock exchange transactions, full service brokers lost a substantial portion of their business to discount brokers who simply handled transactions without providing investment advice.

A new challenge to conventional brokerage operations has been posed by the emergence of the Internet. A company's stock price, financial statements, press releases, etc., are now instantly available to anyone with access to a computer and a modem. Investors registered with an online broker can access additional information and advice about the stocks, and buy or sell shares with almost instant verification.

Despite the forecasts of how rapidly it will grow, e-commerce still represents only about 1 percent of retail sales of physical goods but over one-third of the retail trading of securities is already online. Small wonder that Merrill Lynch announced that it would offer its customers the convenience of instant executions and lower transaction costs, albeit seeking to strengthen its traditional broker services in other ways.

Things are also changing quickly for the stock exchanges, both in this country and elsewhere:

➤ *Combinations.* The National Association of Securities Dealers (NASD) recently merged with the American Stock Exchange (Amex), but Nasdaq (an automated quotation system owned by NASD) and Amex continue to operate and be reported separately. The NASD is pursuing affiliations with a number of stock exchanges in other countries, which could lead to cross trading of listed securities. There have also been efforts to coordinate the operations of the major European stock exchanges by, if nothing else, standardizing the holidays on which trading will not be conducted.

➤ *Extended trading.* Faced with the reality that people want to be able to execute trades after business hours and that new firms can offer this service in one way or another, the stock exchanges are edging towards extended trading hours. Given that some securities are listed for trading in several countries, it would be fair to say that twenty-four-hour trading has arrived.

➤ *Operations.* The idea of a physical location where members meet to trade securities is an anachronism. Although tourists may enjoy seeing capitalism at work, it is far more efficient to match buy and sell orders via computer. The Tokyo Stock Exchange recently closed its trading floor for this reason, and in time the New York Stock Exchange (NYSE) will probably follow suit.

➤ *Organizational form.* The traditional stock exchanges may face growing competition from newly-created electronic trading networks. Plans are afoot to convert both the New York Stock Exchange and Nasdaq from not-for-profit membership organizations to for-profit companies that can more nimbly respond to this challenge.

Obviously, the rapid dissemination of financial information via the Internet could have important effects on how the global financial markets operate, possibly going far beyond the points that have been mentioned. Here is one visionary view expressed in a recent *Business Week* article:

> *At its most basic level, capitalism will work better than ever, thanks to a more efficient and open financial system. The capital markets are a dazzling social and economic institution for communicating all kinds of data, information, and knowledge through price changes. The more pervasive the financial markets, the more investors will find and fund profitable ideas bubbling up from university labs or garages. At the same time, they'll flee from failed management strategies with the click of a mouse.*[4]

Maybe, but a global financial market poses risks as well as opportunities. As the article goes on to say, the market may become more volatile because of the sheer rapidity with which investors can react to disturbing market developments resulting in periodic financial crises. Such volatility could result in the withdrawal of funds by burned investors, driving the cost of capital up rather than down.

Notwithstanding the tremendous impact of the Internet on how things are done, the savvy pros that run the financial markets will be needed as much as ever. The information available to individuals on the Internet may or may not be suitable for making investment decisions. For instance, there are still no internationally recognized standards for reporting the financial results of the companies competing for global capital. Also, the quality of human thought does not necessarily improve as a result of being online; just check out some of the drivel that is posted on electronic bulletin boards for various companies.

CEO: Given the size and complexity of the financial markets, it's probably just as well that there is some governmental oversight.

CFO: I agree, although the national governments are by no means as all-powerful as they once seemed to be.

The financial markets are huge and impersonal, with an ever-present potential for fraud. Two things are essential to keep everyone honest: (1) adequate information about the investments being offered, and (2) reasonable assurances that all concerned will honor their commitments. The case for government involvement is strong, even though private institutions such as stock exchanges can assist in the regulatory process.

Another concern is market turbulence, which if it gets out of hand can result in widespread losses. Thus, even a perfectly sound bank can go under if there is a run on it. Since the 1930s, the United States government has minimized this particular risk by providing mandatory insurance on bank deposits up to certain limits.

What about market disruptions caused by faulty investment decisions? The argument for government intervention is that financial meltdowns are disruptive no matter what causes them.

The flip side is that market participants may develop a "heads I win, tails the Government loses" mindset that will foster even greater imprudence in the future.

> Example: In 1998 there was a near collapse of Long-Term Capital Management LP, a highly leveraged hedge fund with $1.5 billion in capital that was dealing in financial derivatives. Based on computer models, the operation was deemed a "sure thing," but the models failed to consider the possibility of a general drying up of liquidity. The New York Federal Reserve Bank encouraged a bailout by major financial institutions, which was duly executed. It arguably would have been better to allow the principals to lose their capital as an object lesson in the risks of derivatives.

Given the globalization of financial markets, no government has jurisdiction over the entire system. National policies concerning interest rates, money supply, and exchange rates can be quickly frustrated by international capital movements. (The volume of trading in the "foreign exchange" markets is now estimated to be upwards of one *trillion* dollars a day.) An oft-cited example is the "Asian flu" that struck one country after another, both in Asia and elsewhere, after the Thai baht was sharply devalued in July 1997.

Even within a given country, the rapid spread of information via the Internet creates problems for regulators. How can the SEC effectively enforce the ban on trading based on inside information against individuals trading online? What assurance can there be that individual investors will review the company documents that have been filed with and reviewed by the SEC, even though these documents are posted on the Internet for those patient enough to seek them out? Many investors probably pay more attention to press releases and news reports, which are more current and easier to read than the SEC filings, not to mention the information on the so-called "momentum" stock-pick sites.

Some observers rejoice in the limits of government control over the global economy, placing their faith in the "invisible hand" of the financial markets to keep things running properly. Others characterize the situation as out of balance, and complain about the instability of exchange rates, the inequity of global wealth distribution, and the supposedly unchecked power of big companies to play one country off against another in deciding where to locate their investments.

An issue for the future is whether the limitations of national governments can be compensated for by international cooperation, e.g., the periodic meetings of the G-7 countries, or whether international governmental institutions will eventually emerge to fill the gap.

CEO: I presume you would agree that the United States has been dominating the global economy of late.

CFO: That's been true over the past decade, but there is plenty of competition and the situation could change dramatically.

In many respects, the United States has had things pretty much its own way in recent years. To list just a few points:

➤ The *gross domestic product* (GDP) of the United States is the largest of any country on earth, and growing more rapidly than (albeit exceeded by) the combined GDP of the fifteen nations of the European Union.

➤ The United States has run a trade deficit for several decades, consuming more goods and services from elsewhere than it provides to the rest of the world. This has been possible because other countries have invested more heavily in U.S. securities and assets than the United States has invested elsewhere.

➤ There are reportedly more Internet users in the United States than in Europe and Asia combined, signifying a lead in the vitally important information technology sector. Given the size of the world's population and spreading fascination with this new mode of communication, this is not likely to hold true for long.

➣ On June 30, 1999 (according to the *Wall Street Journal*), eight of the ten largest public companies in the world (based on market capitalization) had their headquarters in the United States, namely Microsoft, General Electric, IBM, Wal-Mart, Cisco Systems, Lucent Technologies, Intel, and Exxon.[5]

➣ The United States does not have the biggest banks or insurance companies, but it has played a dominant role in investment banking and other "cutting edge" areas. Those shopping for financial services in London, Tokyo or wherever, will find many familiar names, such as Merrill Lynch, Morgan Stanley Dean Witter, Chase, Citigroup, Pricewaterhouse Coopers, etc.

If the inflow of investment capital dried up and funds started flowing out to the rest of the world, the U.S. dollar and our economic standard of living vis-à-vis the rest of the world could take a major hit. As Burton Malkiel, the author of *A Random Walk Down Wall Street*, recently commented:

> *Only a decade ago we were told that Japanese management techniques were the best in the world, and Japanese stocks soared to unprecedented levels, with the Nikkei index near the 40,000 level. The United States was widely believed to have lost its manufacturing edge, and risk premiums in our market were high. Today the Nikkei index stands at 18,000, and Japan's economy languishes. By contrast, we are described as a supertanker economy that can sail through troubled waters undisturbed. We were not in such bad shape in the 1980s as was supposed, and we may not be so good today.[6]*

Overall, there do not seem to be a lot of warning signs for the U.S. sector of the global economy, but certain companies will surely be tested. Airbus is starting to give Boeing a run for its money, for instance, and Detroit has not heard the last of the Japanese auto companies.

CEO: What's your assessment of this company's prospects?

CFO: Our competitive position seems pretty solid, but there may be problems in attracting the funding needed to become number one in the industry.

CEO: Why should funding be a problem?

CFO: There's lots of money available in the global economy, some $80 trillion of financial assets in fact, but it can go practically anywhere in search of the highest returns—both geographically and from sector to sector. In effect, our company is competing with all the users of capital in the world, including governments.

CEO: I'd like to kick that idea around a bit, but must leave for another meeting shortly. Before we break up, what did you have in mind earlier when you were talking about the enhanced role Finance could play in helping the company meet its goals and objectives?

CFO: I believe Finance is doing a good job in its functional area, by and large, but we could contribute much more to company and business strategy. To get the ball rolling, you and I need to open a dialogue that hasn't existed until now, and work together in an entirely new way.

There are basically four models for a CEO's interactions with the CFO, which in turn will determine the basic relationship between business and Finance people throughout the organization.

➤ The CEO uses the CFO as a "go to" person on tough issues, whether they are financial or not. No major decision reaching the CEO's desk would normally be made without prior consultation with the CFO.

➤ The CEO occasionally calls on the CFO as a sounding board or advisor on business and company matters.

➤ The CEO expects the CFO to take care of the financial affairs of the company and otherwise sees little reason for contact.

➤ The CEO uses the CFO *et al.* as the ramrod for company policies, procedures, and financial objectives.

Unless one of the first two models apply, preferably the first, it will be difficult or impossible for Finance to play an important and positive role in company and business decisions.

CEO: I've got an open mind; we'll talk further. One final question for today: Do you have any suggestions as to what I should tell the board about the earnings outlook?

CFO: There is one thing that may help. Do you remember the litigation reserve that was set up three years ago? We recently updated the analysis based on the current situation and projections, and concluded that most of the money remaining in the reserve will not be needed. Accordingly, it is now timely to make an accounting adjustment. There won't be any tax benefit involved, but the adjustment will legitimately increase current earnings and give the company a fighting chance of hitting the full-year budget.

CEO: Good work, thanks!

SUMMING UP

➤ The business and financial worlds are changing more rapidly than ever before, and they are becoming increasingly competitive.

➤ Since there are never enough resources to go around, every economy requires mechanisms for their allocation. Capitalism or reliance on free markets has emerged as the world's predominant economic model, albeit with significant social constraints.

➤ The advent of new technology (such as the Internet and e-commerce), regional associations, privatization and deregulation are fostering the true globalization of the business and financial markets. Even more remarkable developments can be expected in the 21st century.

➤ Funds available in the global financial markets will flow to whichever organizations offer the best combination of safety and return. All organizations must compete for funds, either directly or indirectly, in this marketplace.

➤ An open dialogue between the CEO and the CFO must exist in order for Finance to take the initiative in helping an organization meet its goals and objectives.

NOTES

1. "A Survey of Europe: A Work in Progress," *Economist*, 23 October 1999. © 1999 The Economist Newspaper Group, Inc. Reprinted with permission. Further reproduction prohibited. www.economist.com
2. Kenichi Ohmae, *The Borderless World: Power and Strategy in the Interlinked Economy*, revised edition (New York: HarperBusiness/HarperCollins Publishers, 1999), 18. Copyright © 1991 by McKinsey & Co., Inc. Reprinted by permission of HarperCollins Publishers, Inc.
3. Peter F. Drucker, "Beyond the Information Revolution," *Atlantic Monthly*, October 1999, 50.
4. Christopher Farrell, "All the World's an Auction Now," *Business Week*, 4 October 1999.
5. *Wall Street Journal*, special section on world business, 27 September 1999, R30.
6. Burton G. Malkiel, "How Much Higher Can the Market Go," *Wall Street Journal*, 22 September 1999.

Chapter Two

SEEKING SHAREHOLDER VALUE

The engine which drives Enterprise is not Thrift, but Profit.

John Maynard Keynes, 1930

CEO: I've been thinking about the global capital market, and it doesn't seem like such a big deal after all. Although this company should obviously minimize its interest expense, I suspect there is more potential for cost savings in other areas.

CFO: The company's after-tax interest rate is currently about 6 percent, which admittedly doesn't seem too bad, but it could soar if our debt rating deteriorated or inflation started heating up again. What's really important is the cost of our equity, which is much higher than the cost of borrowing.

There is a tendency to think of money markets and equity markets as separate and distinct, with one being rather stodgy (e.g., interest rates are up half a percentage point since the beginning of the year) and the other quite volatile (e.g., the Dow fell over one hundred points yesterday). Bear in mind, however, that the funds available for investment can go into either debt instruments or stock.

The actions of the Federal Reserve Board only directly affect interest rates, but stock markets are said to react to the subtlest hint from Alan Greenspan, Federal Reserve chairman, as to the course of future monetary policy. Likewise, interest rates can move well outside the normal range during periods of economic instability.

Back in the late 1970s, the stock market was in the doldrums. The NYSE common stock index at the end of 1978 had declined some 15 percent over the past six years, and was only slightly higher than it had been at the end of 1965. *Business Week* captured the prevailing stock market pessimism in a cover story on "The Death of Equities." Meanwhile, interest rates were soaring because of escalating inflation.

Short-term interest rates spiked to 20 percent or so in 1980 and 1981. Although long-term rates did not go as high, many bondholders were earning negative returns after inflation. It seemed that the United States might be headed for the type of hyperinflation and high interest rates that have plagued certain Latin American countries.

While the Federal Reserve Board under Paul Volcker (appointed chairman in mid-1979) was trying to fight inflation with monetary policy, fiscal policy was going the other way as Federal government deficits ramped up because President Reagan's tax cut was enacted without a corresponding reduction in government spending.

Monetary policy won, and short-term interest rates fell to more normal levels, but many basically sound companies continued to have trouble obtaining longer-term financing. Enter Michael Milken and his associates at Drexel Burnham, who built a lucrative business out of arranging "junk bond" financing at premium interest rates for lower tier companies.

Borrowing is generally easier today, but there can be no assurance that the good times will continue. Despite the overall strong tone of the U.S. economy, there has been a worrisome increase in borrowing defaults. If the trend continues, many companies could find themselves paying substantially higher interest rates.

If a company defaults and its assets are liquidated, the lenders will have priority over the shareholders as to the proceeds. Lenders typically demand a substantial equity cushion, so that the shareholders will have an incentive to see to it that they are paid.

CEO: I realize that equity is far more expensive than debt, but our company has no foreseeable need to sell stock, and the dividend payout is only 2 percent of our market capitalization. Therefore, what practical difference does the cost of equity make?

CFO: Whether the company plans to sell stock or not, we need to keep the shareholders happy. Shareholders aren't simply looking to dividends for a return; they also expect growth in the stock price.

Shareholders assume far more risk than bondholders, banks, and other lenders. They have no guarantee that the current dividend will continue to be paid, let alone that their principal will be recovered. Accordingly, it stands to reason that they expect to earn a higher—not lower—rate of return than lenders. Basically, there are two ways they can get higher rates:

1. Most companies try not only to maintain but also to increase their dividends over time. A cut in the dividend generally indicates weakness, whereas a dividend increase demonstrates confidence in the future.

Dividend payout rates in recent years have been held down by the popularity of stock repurchase programs, which is an alternative way to return money to the shareholders that is more tax efficient. Shareholders are given a choice: They can either take cash or hold on to their stock with the expectation that it will increase in value when the number of shares outstanding is reduced.

2. The stock price can be expected to increase over time if there is growth in underlying earnings and cash flow. That will not necessarily hold true for every company or for the market as a whole in a particular year, but equity investors have fared quite well over the longer term.

Consider the dramatic increases in the S&P 500 and other major U.S. stock price indices in recent years; stock prices cannot continue increasing more than 20 percent per year when earnings and cash flow are not growing nearly as fast, but still it has been quite a run.

CEO: Obviously, the shareholders will benefit if the stock price goes up, but where's the cost to the company?

CFO: There isn't a cash outlay *per se*, unless the stock price increase happens to reflect share repurchases, but such increases aren't something that just happens. In effect we're on a treadmill, with the shareholders demanding continually improving results that will support growth in the stock price or—to use the buzzword—increase shareholder value.

Various things can upset the status quo if shareholder expectations aren't met. For example, one of the company's competitors or a leveraged buyout group might be emboldened by our relatively low stock price to make a takeover bid.

Offering a premium over the market price of the target company is logical because:

> ➤ The combined company (the acquiring company and the target company) could operate more profitably, by eliminating excess capacity or redundant support functions.
> ➤ The takeover group has a plan to restructure the target company and unleash untapped shareholder value.

The board of the target company may agree that acceptance of the offer is in the best interests of the shareholders, in which case the acquisition can go through quickly as long as no antitrust objection is raised. Key managers in the target company often find themselves out of a job, which may not be so painful if their company has previously provided for "golden parachute" payments.

In other cases, the board of the target company will resist on grounds that the price being offered is inadequate, and that the corporate strategy in place will make more of a contribution to shareholder value in the long run than that of the takeover group.

There may be defensive measures in place already to ward off an unwelcome bid, such as:

➤ staggered boards, i.e., a percentage of the board faces election each year, which can delay the seizure of control through a proxy contest

➤ required supermajority stockholder approval for a merger of the company or for a purchase of its assets that is not endorsed by management

➤ "poison pills" or rights granted to the existing shareholders to purchase additional stock at a sharp discount under certain conditions

Another defensive strategy is to find a "white knight" willing to enter the fray, either in hopes of raising the ante or because the new entrant is viewed as a better fit.

Example: Following the unsolicited Seagram bid for Conoco in June 1981, DuPont made a higher offer with the encouragement of Conoco's management. A bidding contest ensued in which a third company joined. Ultimately, Mobil made the highest bid, but it was contingent on government approvals that had not yet been obtained, whereas DuPont was ready to close the deal.

DuPont's winning bid was nearly $8 billion in cash and stock, which was at the time the largest acquisition (in dollars) on record. By allowing the Conoco shares that it had acquired during the battle to be converted into DuPont stock, Seagram wound up with a 23 percent interest in DuPont.

How things can change! By the end of the 1990s, Seagram sold its stake back to DuPont to fund investments in the entertainment sector. DuPont divested Conoco while expanding its involvement in biotechnology. The consolidation trend in the oil industry continued, and a massive combination of Exxon and Mobil has taken place.

Then there is the so-called "Pac-Man defense," with the target company making a counter bid for the would-be acquirer.

Example: Elf Acquitaine recently attempted to ward off a bid from another French oil company named TotalFina using this tactic. At stake was not only who would be reporting to whom after the merger, but also whether the combined chemical operations would be retained as part of the merged company or spun off as a separate entity.

After a two-month standoff, an agreement was reached that TotalFina would acquire Elf Acquitaine as originally proposed, thereby forming the world's fourth largest oil company. To obtain Elf Acquitaine's acceptance of the takeover, TotalFina increased its all-share bid by 9 percent and agreed to equal representation of the two companies on the combined company's board.

Other possible defenses include bargaining with the would-be acquirer to accept a "greenmail" payment and the "just say no" defense.

CEO: So long as management is trying to do the right thing, they should at least be able to count on support from their company's own shareholders.

CFO: That isn't necessarily true, because the shareholders tend to view management as being inbred or self-interested.

There was a time when equity capital was relatively patient. Stocks were typically bought and held for the long term by pension funds, mutual funds, and individual investors. It was recognized that stock prices could fall as well as rise.

Fluctuations in the stock price were considered beyond management's control, and diversification was seen as the key to minimizing portfolio risk. If investors became disillusioned with a particular investment, they would quietly sell it and buy something else.

The market psychology is quite different today, perhaps because fewer market participants have ever experienced a real bear market. There has been a tendency to make equity investments with an increasingly short time horizon in mind, as manifested by the "day trading" craze.

Approximately half of all U.S. households now own equity securities, either directly or through pension and mutual funds, and a recent study concluded that small-time, individual investors continue to subscribe to the "buy-and-hold" investment strategy. Other studies indicate, however, that the stocks of many companies—including such well-known names as AT&T, General Motors, IBM, and Microsoft—are turning over with increasing rapidity. Reportedly, some 76 percent of the shares of the average NYSE company were traded in 1998, as compared to 46 percent in 1990 and 12 percent in 1960.[1]

When stock price setbacks do occur, investors seem less and less inclined to suffer in silence. Indeed, some very large stockholders have taken to pressuring management for remedial action.

> Example: The California Public Employees' Retirement System (CalPERS) funds health and retirement benefits for over one million state and local employees. Viewing its role as that of a shareowner rather than shareholder, CalPERS compiles an annual focus list of companies which it considers to be laggards because of sub-par stock price performance, poor financial results, or questionable corporate governance practices.
>
> CalPERS has followed up by submitting shareholder proposals for elimination or prohibition of many of the antitakeover defenses previously discussed. It also pushes for more outside directors, the formation of shareholder advisory committees, and corporate initiatives to improve performance. The giant fund does not always get its way, but one would suspect that they are not often turned away without a hearing.

Whether it is called "downsizing" or "rightsizing," a corporate restructuring plan generally boils down to divesting assets, closing operations, and/or slashing overhead and operational costs. There may be a big initial charge for retirement and severance costs, which is identified as an abnormal item for reporting purposes and tends to be quickly forgotten by investors. As a result, the earnings over the next few quarters are usually inflated by the cost reductions, albeit with potentially negative results on the revenue base.

All in all, corporate restructuring is generally a plus in the long term. The willingness of U.S. companies to bite the bullet in the late 1980s and early 1990s quite possibly explains the revival of U.S. economic competitiveness in the global economy. More recently, there has been an increasing tendency to follow suit in other countries. Even Japanese companies have been edging away from their vaunted commitment to "lifetime employment."

Restructuring is far from a panacea, however, and there are failures as well as successes.

> Example: Al Dunlap developed a reputation as a corporate turnaround manager, based on his dramatic interventions at a series of companies. At Scott Paper, for instance, he presided over a drastic cutback program followed by a quick sale of the company with results that delighted the shareholders.
>
> At Sunbeam Corporation, Dunlap again took drastic action. The restructuring plan that was approved by the board called for eliminating half of the company's employees and the majority of its products.
>
> The plan backfired, leaving Sunbeam with a demoralized organization, declining revenues, and financial difficulties. Dunlap was fired by the board, the independent accountants were replaced, and the financial results were restated for several prior periods.

Resistance to a failed takeover offer is sometimes attributed to the job security concerns of one or two key executives, which makes corporate leaders seem inbred and self-interested. The prevalence of "golden parachute" plans in large U.S. companies has developed, at least in part, to encourage corporate leaders to let go in such situations.

Another cause of dissatisfaction with top executives is the perception that they are sometimes richly compensated for leading their companies to mediocre results. Some suggestions for avoiding such a result will be offered later.

CEO: All right. How much is our cost of equity?

CFO: Based on current market information, the company's cost of equity is about 13 percent. Blending that figure with the cost of borrowing and our planned debt ratio, our overall cost of capital is 12 percent.

The cost of equity is typically estimated as the sum of the current yield on long-term Treasury bonds, which is taken to represent a "risk free" return, and an equity risk premium based on the long-term historical spread between equity returns and Treasury bond yields and on the company's market volatility. The cost of capital is then calculated based on the estimated costs of equity and borrowing, and an assumed debt ratio. For further details, see Appendix A.

Given the assumptions involved, the cost of capital represents an estimate that at best is accurate within a percentage point or two. Nevertheless, this benchmark provides a rational linkage between a company's internal financial data and the capital markets, which seems far better than flying by the seat of one's pants.

The projected cash outflows and inflows from a proposed investment can be discounted to present value at the cost of capital. In theory, a company should undertake all investments that offer a positive Net Present Value (NPV), whereas investments with negative NPV should be rejected.

Two other measures of investment merit offer additional perspectives that may be useful, namely:

1. *Internal Rate of Return* (IRR)—permits alternative investment proposals to be ranked on a return basis as well as assessed vis-a-vis the cost of capital.
2. *Discounted Payback* (DP)—indicates how long funds will be at risk on a discounted cash flow basis, which may be of great importance if the useful economic life of an investment is expected to be relatively short.

Appendix B explains and illustrates NPV, IRR, and DP calculations using a hypothetical project.

CEO: So you're saying that this company needs to provide a return to shareholders of 12 percent, year after year?

CFO: Exactly, which would mean the shareholders would have to triple the value of their investment every ten years.

CEO: That seems unrealistic in our industry.

CFO: If the growth isn't there, the company will need to get into new lines of business or return money to the shareholders rather than reinvesting it disadvantageously.

To appreciate what a 12 percent cost of capital means, one must consider the power of compounding over an extended period of time. To begin with, assume a company is reinvesting all of its cash flow so the shareholders are looking solely to stock price increases for their return.

Tripling the stock price in ten years may seem doable if opportunities to improve the company's strategies or operations are perceived. It is harder to visualize how such a rate of increase can be sustained over the long term. Note the 12 percent growth rate column in Table 2–1.

By the end of twenty years, the stock price should be nearly ten times the base level, which begins to sound pretty difficult, and the stock price target after fifty years is almost 300 times the initial price.

One common reaction to numbers such as these is that the cost of capital has been somehow overstated, which may be true.

Table 2-1. One dollar compounded at X percent for indicated
periods.

Cumulative Years	Growth Rate			
	12%	9%	6%	3%
0	1.0	1.0	1.0	1.0
10	3.1	2.4	1.8	1.3
20	9.6	5.6	3.2	1.8
30	30.0	13.3	5.7	2.4
40	93.1	31.4	10.3	3.3
50	289.0	74.4	18.4	4.4

The estimation procedure (described in Appendix A) is subject to many questions, such as the following:

➤ The *historical* data on which the cost of capital is based are not necessarily predictive of the future. Since it is unclear what information should be used to estimate future cost of capital, it is difficult to know whether the cost of capital should be higher or lower than estimates based on historical data.

➤ It arguably "mixes apples and oranges" to add *historical* debt versus equity yield differential to the *current* Treasury bond yield. If the cost of equity was simply equated with *historical* equity yields, the estimated cost of capital would currently be reduced by about one percentage point.

➤ The cost of capital is estimated on a nominal rate basis, including inflation (which in the United States has averaged around 3 percent per year over the past seventy-five years). With zero inflation, the indicated cost of capital would be reduced by about three percentage points. If inflation in the United States heats up, e.g., because of depreciation of the U.S. dollar vis-à-vis other currencies driving up the price of imported goods, then current cost of capital estimates may be understated.

A cost of capital in the 10–12 percent range may be suitable for many companies under current conditions. Even if such an estimate was deemed to be on the high side, a modest degree of conservatism could be useful as an offset to shortfalls in actual versus forecast results. (See the subsequent discussion of hurdle rates.)

A company may find it exceedingly difficult to triple its value every ten years if the industry in which it is competing has limited growth prospects. Efficiency gains and increasing market share can take a company only so far. There are, however, several possible solutions:

1. Return some money to the shareholders via dividends, thereby reducing the required growth to a more manageable level. (Alternatively, buy back stock and reduce the number of shares that need to appreciate in value.) A company that pays a 3 percent dividend, for instance, should only be expected to increase its share price by 2.4 times over ten years (see the 9 percent column in the Table 2–1). Thus, a relatively modest dividend payout could reduce the stock-price growth requirement by approximately 25 percent.

2. Reinvent the business so as to enhance the opportunity for profitable growth. The key is to reconsider your assumptions as to customer needs and wants.

Example: By dint of strenuous and persistent efforts, Yamaha captured 40 percent of the global piano market, only to realize that the overall demand for pianos had started to decline by 10 percent per year, and South Korean piano producers were coming on line in a bid for the low end of the market. What could Yamaha do?

Yamaha's managers took a hard look at the situation, and realized that there were 40 million pianos in the world, many of which were sitting around idle, neglected, and out of tune, because fewer and fewer people had the time or inclination to learn to play them.

The key to creating value for customers, therefore, was not selling more new pianos, but finding a way to add value to the millions of pianos already out there. Yamaha's answer was to marry new technology with the traditional player piano. Now dust-collecting pieces of oversized furniture can be retrofitted so that great artists can play the piano for owners in the privacy of their homes. This new technology created the prospect of a $2,500 sale to the owners of all those idle pianos, plus the potential of marketing software recordings and tuning services—not bad for a "declining industry."[2]

3. **Migrate from the existing business into new activities offering greater potential for growth.** In recent years, there has been a massive transfer of capital and human talent into perceived growth industries, such as the Internet, telecommunications, and biotechnology, while many traditional manufacturing and services businesses are stagnating. There will be major rewards for those who can figure out how to reposition their businesses on the leading as opposed to bleeding edge of change.

Example: The U.S. network television business is on the decline, reflecting inroads by cable TV, the saturation of programming with commercials (at some point, viewers will surely rebel), and the appeal of advertising and promotion on the Internet (permits more targeted approaches and reaches a worldwide audience).

Seeing the handwriting on the wall, Mel Karmazin of CBS found a variety of ways to exchange the network franchise for investments in other businesses with more potential. Thus, Karmazin invested in several Internet sites, paying with commercial airtime on CBS instead of cash. Then he negotiated a deal for CBS to be acquired by Viacom, an entertainment conglomerate with interests in motion pictures, cable TV, television programming, publishing, and more, creating what was described as the "world's premier entertainment and media company." [3]

4. **Remember that fortune does not favor the faint of heart. When the situation requires, be prepared to move fast and catch the wave.**

Example: In 1998, Nortel Networks, Canada's largest high-technology company, acquired Bay Networks, a California maker of Internet gear, for stock valued at $7 billion. The deal was perceived unfavorably by securities analysts at first, but opinions changed when it became evident that Nortel's revenues would grow nearly 30 percent in 1999 with a larger percentage increase in earnings. The key to these results was being a player in the exploding market for Internet networking systems, competing head to head with the likes of Cisco Systems and Lucent Technologies.

According to CEO John Roth, the bet was one that Nortel had to take. The alternative was remaining simply a traditional voice-communications equipment supplier, with "an absolute certainty of going out of business."[4]

Such success stories notwithstanding, earning a 12 percent cash return is not easy over the long term. Many companies fail and lose control of their destinies, while new firms are constantly coming into existence. Are there any companies listed on the New York Stock Exchange that are in the same business they were one hundred years ago?

CEO: Our company has found that forecast investment returns are almost invariably overstated. Therefore, wouldn't it be a good idea to anticipate investment shortfalls by setting hurdle rates that reflect the applicable risk? We could require 15 percent for cost reduction projects, 20 percent for expansion projects, and 25 percent for new endeavors outside our field of expertise.

CFO: I understand where you're coming from, but hurdle rates in excess of the cost of capital would penalize honest project forecasts. More hyping of project returns could be expected, with even greater shortfalls in actual versus forecast results than at present. Alternatively, the use of hurdle rates would remove many good investment proposals from consideration, which would also be unfortunate. In theory, at least, all projects with a return in excess of the cost of capital should be undertaken. Granted, project risk must be addressed in some manner, but I believe there are better ways to do so.

In theory, any investment proposal (or project) that will return the cost of capital can be financed through a combination of debt and equity financing. The future is unpredictable, however, and the assumptions used in evaluating projects will often be wide of the mark.

The cost of capital includes an equity risk premium appropriate for a company's overall operations. It does not provide for the greater than average risks associated with certain projects, e.g., endeavors outside the company's field of expertise. This raises the question of how to deal with project risk.

One common approach is to use various discount rates depending on the nature of the project, e.g., a series of hurdle rates ranging from 15 to 25 percent. The specific rates tend to be subjective, and some projects will not fit neatly into the established categories. How would a project be classified, for instance, that was aimed at reducing costs but involved the use of revolutionary new technology with which the company had no experience?

Whether driven by corporate management or Finance, the use of varying discount rates to evaluate projects that are competing for funding is likely to frustrate businesspeople. After all, what value can they have for seemingly arbitrary hurdle rates based on judgments in which they played no part? As the *Economist* put it in a recent article, "in practice, setting discount rates at the right level is almost impossible," and "real-life managers" tend not to like the discounted cash flow approach "for the simple reason that it ignores the value of real-life managers."[5]

It would hardly be surprising if some project advocates responded by hyping forecast results to surmount whatever hurdle rate had been imposed. Another response might be to contend that favored projects were "strategic," and therefore should be approved without regard to cost justification.

Thus, a procedure adopted with the best of intentions could impede honest dialogue about the merits of investment proposals vying for approval. As will be discussed later, a better approach is available. If the businesspeople get involved in assessing project risks, they will have far more value for the results. Look for the problem of project shortfalls to be substantially reduced.

CEO: Your points are well taken, but I still believe that my rates represent the kind of safety margin the company should be looking for. Also, I simply can't agree that all projects with returns in excess of the cost of capital should be undertaken. How does that square with our capital constraints, such as the debt ratio that the board wants to maintain?

CFO: Many people would agree with you. Most companies consider themselves subject to capital constraints, which if nothing else represents a good way to preserve some financial flexibility. The required rates of return that you mentioned seem pretty high to me, but they shouldn't do any harm so long as they aren't publicized or rigidly enforced. Given that all proposed projects are evaluated on the basis of IRR as well as NPV, the higher return projects will typically be chosen anyway.

CEO: OK. Now here's another question. We forecast incremental returns for investment proposals, but a business must be run on an overall basis. Suppose a process improvement at a buggy whip plant offers a return of 40 percent, but the overall operation is doomed?

CFO: That illustrates the perils of tunnel vision. It's essential to consider the total business perspective in setting up the alternative to a proposed investment, because going out of business may be the true base case as opposed to continuing the present operation.

It is a fact of life that many once flourishing industries have become obsolete. Thus, no business can make much of a profit on buggy whips when almost everyone is driving automobiles. At most, there may be room for one producer to satisfy requests from nostalgia buffs.

Other industries experience waves of consolidation in which the strongest players expand while the laggards are absorbed, go under, or survive in market niches.

Example: Look what has been happening to U.S. banks, as the barriers to interstate banking operations are being dismantled and investment brokers and others are attracting a growing share of total financial assets by offering such services as money market accounts. Thousands of banks have disappeared in mergers and acquisitions over the past decade, and the top five U.S. banks' share of total bank assets has approximately doubled (to about 20 percent, which is still low by international standards). The likely end result is not a half dozen U.S. banks, for many small banks will be able to thrive by offering distinctive services, but the current population of 9,000 U.S. banks will continue to dwindle.

On the other hand, there is an explosion of entrants in emerging industries. Consider all the companies being spawned by the rapid evolution of the Internet from a toy for techies to a business and household necessity. Many "dot com" companies will fall by the wayside, but some of the survivors will make it big.

No business can do it all. There may be some things that employees know how to do superlatively, other things that they can learn, and many things that someone else could do better.

Businesses in the corporate portfolio may be more profitable as a separate operation or under different management. In such cases, shareholder value can be enhanced by divesting it. On the other hand, acquisitions can help to build up the businesses on which a company plans to focus.

Similarly, someone else could probably handle some company functions more efficiently. Whether it is cleaning the offices or running the computer network, outsourcing is often the way to go.

CEO: Looking at things from a shareholder value perspective, shouldn't our internal evaluations of investments and businesses be based on their effect on the company's earnings. After all, that's what the financial statements emphasize, and I doubt the securities analysts and investors pay much attention to cash flow.

CFO: We do get more questions from the investment community about the earnings outlook. Nevertheless, I believe that cash flow is a better predictor of future market value. Earnings reflect many judgments, such as FIFO (first-in-first-out) versus LIFO (last-in-first-out) inventory methods, capitalizing or expensing certain disbursements, etc., whereas cash is simply what's left over after collecting from customers and paying employees, suppliers, etc. In other words, cash is a hard number with no adjustments or estimates.

Earnings and cash flow for any business will be equal in the long run, but over shorter periods the conventions used for earnings purposes provide a distorted picture of economic reality. For instance:

➤ A sale is not really a sale until the customer pays the bill, but it is accrued for the income statement when the product is shipped or the service is provided.

➤ The economic cost of a piece of equipment is borne when it is bought and paid for, not as the asset is amortized over a period of time that is not even necessarily representative of its useful life.

➤ Increases or decreases in working capital can have a major impact on the company's cash position, yet they are not reflected in the income statement at all.

➤ Deferred tax accounting gets so involved that you can meet yourself coming and going. The important thing is how much money is currently being paid out for taxes.

To be fair about it, cash flow data can be confusing too. Net cash flow may be the true "bottom line" for a mature business, but a cash inflow (cash flow before capital expenditures) perspective is more useful for a rapidly growing business with heavy initial investment requirements.

Example: AT&T acquired McCaw Cellular for about $12 billion. At the time, McCaw had never reported an operating profit. McCaw did offer substantial cash inflow, as well as a wireless telephone capability that would have taken AT&T considerable time and money to develop internally. Thus, a company without earnings can have a high market value if it has a strong potential cash flow.

Beyond the judgments with earnings data, you also need to consider the investment base. Suppose that Company A's market capitalization (outstanding shares × stock price) equals stock-holder's equity while Company B's stock is trading at three times its stockholder's equity. Comparing the respective returns on equity (ROE) of these companies would ignore the shareholder perspective, because shareholders measure their returns based on market values—not book values. Thus, while the ROE for Company A equals its return on market (or economic) value, the ROE for Company B is three times higher than its return on market value.

There are many smart people participating in the securities markets, all of whom are trying to make money. Certainly, the valuations that result from their collective actions are less than perfect, but it is hard to believe that market valuations will not tend to come into balance with intrinsic economic values over the long run.

When one or two savvy investors or analysts figure out that a company's stock, or the stocks in a specific sector, or the market as a whole is valued too high or too low, there can quickly be an adjustment. That is what Joel Stern and Bennett Stewart, two leading exponents of shareholder value techniques, were getting at when they coined the expression "lead steer" investor.

CEO: Maybe it would be easier to head up a government agency or nonprofit organization, and not have to worry about pleasing the shareholders.

CFO: They've got their problems attracting fundings, too.

At first glance, the market-driven performance model only seems to apply to business firms. There is no obvious parallel to earning the cost of capital for an organization that exists to spend money for purposes that are deemed essential or useful.

Indeed, it can be argued that a government agency has an incentive to nurture the problems that it was created to address rather than solving them. As columnist George Melloan put it:

> *The incentive systems in government and private businesses differ, which is why, on the whole, private enterprises are better at solving problems than government. Putting it bluntly, the incentive in government is to preserve the problem and thereby preserve bureaucratic power and bureaucratic jobs.*

In addition, he said:

> *Their goal is best achieved by demonstrating, often through skillful manipulation of a gullible press, that some crisis—drug usage, starving children, dying butterflies—is so terrible that only a cold, unfeeling legislator would vote against additional taxpayer money.*[6]

Remember, though, that there is a limit to the amount of money that a government can raise through taxes or borrow before the national economy stagnates or the voters rebel. Also, government agencies compete with each other for the available supply of funds. Political support is often fickle, and the agencies that thrive in the long run will be the ones that find ways to ensure that their programs provide benefits that genuinely outweigh the costs.

Experience shows that the assessment process cannot be effectively conducted from the outside. Consider what happened when the Grace Commission undertook a private sector review of Federal government expenditures in the 1980s. Sweeping spending cuts were recommended, but the voluminous study results were little noticed and soon forgotten.

Thus, government agencies should borrow techniques from the private sector in an effort to ensure that their programs add value. Here are some of the possibilities:

➤ Fund some government programs (e.g., parks) by user fees as opposed to taxes so that the specific beneficiaries will pay for the program rather than taxpayer generally. Willingness to pay is powerful evidence that the benefit of a government program is real, and not merely something that people take because it is "free."

➤ Compare cost to benefits where such an analysis is meaningful. Such studies have long been made by agencies such as the U.S. Army Corps of Engineers in evaluating proposed water resource investments.

➤ Include an allowance for the time value of money when the present value of expenditures is being compared to the future value of anticipated benefits. The current yield on long-term Treasury bonds is probably an appropriate discount rate for the government as opposed to the cost of capital for a business firm.

➤ Eliminate organizational layers and delegate more authority to the working level. This improves both the efficiency and effectiveness of an agency's operations, and therefore will serve the public better.

➤ Institute appropriate incentives to reward superior individual and team performance.

➤ Outsource operations that can be more effectively or economically conducted by other organizations.

➤ Emulate the "spin-off" technique by splitting agencies with disparate operations that could be better evaluated and conducted on a stand-alone basis.

Finance is often an underutilized asset and resource in the business world (as will be discussed), and this is also true in the public sector. Rather than spending most of their time double-checking expense vouchers and such, the people in government who are financially trained could be helping the operating people put cost-saving ideas into practice.

Nonprofit organizations (universities, churches, social welfare agencies, cultural organizations, etc.) are in a similar situation. There are distinct limits to the available pool of funds, and many worthy programs must compete for funding. Like a business, they must attract sufficient funds (grants, donations, fees, etc.) to carry out their purposes. Without adequate funding, no matter how worthwhile their purposes, they will not survive. Once again, their Finance people can help to effectively utilize the resources that are available and thereby attract continuing funding.

CEO: Back to the problem at hand, the company's stock price is down 20 percent this month, but it's still the same company that it was last month. Who says the market is necessarily right?

CFO: That's a valid question, but the price drop shouldn't be taken lightly. Some things need to be tightened up in our operations, and a failure to take corrective action could prove very costly.

CEO: So, what are you suggesting should be done?

CFO: I'm not convinced we need a corporate restructuring, although it could come to that. Many things could be accomplished just by unleashing the power of financial thinking in the company to create shareholder value. I guarantee you it will give us a competitive advantage.

CEO: You've got my attention. Let's get together again next week, and you can explain what you have in mind.

Summing Up

➣ The global financial markets are a reality. There will be no long-term survival for organizations, no matter how worthy their purposes, unless they obtain sufficient funding in these markets.

➣ Equity investors have become increasingly demanding about stock price performance in the here-and-now.

➣ Industry consolidations and restructurings are accelerating in response to such demands.

➣ If shareholder value is not created—and every resource is not used effectively—the growth and very survival of any organization is at risk.

➤ Proposed investments to increase shareholder value should be compared to the cost of capital using discounted cash flow procedures, but the overall business outlook and applicable risks must also be taken into account.

NOTES

1. John A. Byrne, "When Capital Gets Antsy: How Stock Churning Is Reshaping Corporate America," *Business Week*, 13 September 1999.
2. Kenichi Ohmae, *The Borderless World: Power and Strategy in the Interlinked Economy*, revised edition (New York: HarperBusiness/ HarperCollins Publishers, 1999), 39–42. Copyright © 1991 by McKinsey & Co., Inc. Reprinted by permission of HarperCollins Publishers, Inc.
3. Viacom press release, September 7, 1999.
4. Mark Heinzl, "Nortel Networks Is Following a Daring Strategy to Recast the Business for Internet Commerce," *Wall Street Journal*, 1 November 1999.
5. "Keeping All Options Open," *Economist*, 14 August 1999. © 1999 The Economist Newspaper Group, Inc. Reprinted with permission. Further reproduction prohibited. www.economist.com
6. George Melloan, "'Save the Problem!' Is the Battle Cry of Bureaucrats," *Wall Street Journal*, 31 August 1999.

Chapter Three

THE POWER OF BETTER FINANCIAL THINKING

Mind is the great lever of all things; human thought is the process by which all human needs are ultimately answered.

Daniel Webster, 1825

CEO: Today's topic is better financial thinking. What exactly do you mean by that?

CFO: All organizations must compete for funding and there are stiff penalties for those that don't make the cut. They—or their constituent business units, functions, or people—can expect to be downsized, outsourced, divested, or otherwise eliminated.

Better financial thinking is about seeking the most productive ways to cope with this reality so that the organization will have a competitive advantage and be able to attain its objectives. Contrary to popular opinion, such a mindset is not necessarily obvious, simplistic, or myopic.

To illustrate what better financial thinking is all about, consider the following problem: Product X persistently loses money. The knee-jerk reaction might be that the losses cannot be allowed to continue, ergo the product must be discontinued or divested, but many other possibilities exist:

1. Perhaps there is some way to restore Product X to profitability by reducing costs, which does not necessarily involve internal cutbacks. Many companies have enjoyed success in paring back their suppliers and service providers, and negotiating price concessions with the firms with which they continue to do business.

2. There could also be a problem with the company's cost allocation procedures. Consequently, Product X results are being burdened by costs more properly charged to other operations.

> Example: One of the cutting-edge financial techniques of recent years, activity-based costing, reflects the premise that costs should be assigned to revenue streams based on usage or effort. This can readily be done for raw materials and direct labor costs, but it is more difficult for indirect costs (supporting services). Traditionally, indirect costs were allocated based on sales, investment, etc., which seemed fine so long as they represented a relatively small percentage of total costs.
>
> In an increasingly knowledge-based economy, indirect costs account for an ever larger share of total costs, which magnifies the distortions from statistical allocations. Activity-based costing attempts to redress the balance by identifying what is really driving the indirect costs and assigning them accordingly.

Assume that an activity-based cost study shows that Product Z, which until now was believed to have a very attractive profit margin, is unprofitable, whereas Product X is modestly profitable. Although Product Z has been bearing only 5 percent of the cost of the technical support group, over half of that group's effort goes to support it.

Once the cost picture has been clarified, a realistic assessment can be made as to what action to take. Perhaps the solution will turn out to be increasing the Product Z selling price, or billing out technical service in excess of specified levels. In either case, Product X may also still need some attention.

3. On the revenue side, it is possible that marketing could identify new markets for Product X that would restore it to profitability and obviate the need for internal cutbacks. There also might be a case for adjusting the Product X selling price, either up if this is competitively possible, or down if the resulting reduction in per unit revenue could be more than made up on additional volume.

4. Another twist would be that although Product X is losing money, it is still covering all of its variable costs and helping to cover unavoidable fixed costs (e.g., maintenance of a rail line) that contribute to the profitability of other products. Under such circumstances, it might be appropriate to temporarily continue producing and selling Product X at a modest loss while continuing to keep a careful eye on the situation and look for better long-term solutions, i.e., a company must not increment itself to death.

Perhaps Product X is a sophisticated new product in an embryonic industry with explosive growth potential. Heavy costs are being incurred for technical improvements and market penetration, resulting in current losses, but such costs will be easily covered by increased sales volume in the future if the product can be turned into a winner. Indeed, it might actually be justifiable to reduce its price significantly (thereby increasing current losses) if that is what it takes to penetrate the market.

The logic of accepting initial losses is reflected in the trendy "lifecycle costing" concept, which basically means trying to anticipate how costs and revenues will play out over a product's lifetime. Lifecycle costing may be appropriate, if not inevitable, for Internet start-ups, new pharmaceutical products, and other products based on leading edge technology. Success is not guaranteed when a company "bets the ranch," however, and there will be losers as well as winners. Technology leaders should watch out for "fast followers," and be prepared to change course if and when the situation requires.

Example: Iridium created a satellite-based wireless communication system of unmatched technological sophistication, but in the process, they incurred development costs of five billion dollars with an additional one billion dollars per year required to operate the system. The explosive growth of wireless phones had demonstrated the potential for this bet to pay off big.

Unfortunately, Iridium's handset cost $3,000 and weighed a pound, and the system did not work inside buildings or cars. Airtime prices ranged from four to nine dollars a minute. No wonder most of the potential customers opted for alternative systems that were more affordable, weighed less, and were more convenient.

Iridium recently declared bankruptcy, as did rival ICO Global Communications Ltd. Even ignoring the development costs, it seems unlikely that Iridium will be able to cover its operating costs in the foreseeable future. That would require one million customers paying $1,000 per year, when their 1999 subscriber base was only 20,000.

5. Finally, the knee-jerk reaction that was mentioned at the outset may be right after all. Perhaps Product X cannot be restored to acceptable profitability and the company would be better off without it. If that is what the analysis shows, there should be no hesitation in discontinuing the product and redeploying the resources it was consuming.

There is no way to identify the best answer without more information, but better financial thinking has shown that even a relatively simple problem like losses on a particular product can have a wide range of possible solutions.

CEO: You said earlier that the company needs to cover its cost of capital, but how can we determine whether this is being done with internal financial data?

CFO: One approach is to track return on investment which isn't really comparable to the cost of capital, but at least reflects the fact that there is a cost for money tied up in a business. Some decisions need to be made, such as how ROI will be calculated, how investments will be allocated, and what level of return can be considered satisfactory.

Net present value provides a more direct link to the cost of capital, but requires periodic valuations of business units that may be somewhat subjective. Despite these weaknesses, there is much to be said for using both of these tools to measure business performance.

There are various ways to calculate return on book asset values, none of which will yield returns that are truly comparable to the cost of capital. An immediate issue is assigning assets that are used in common, such as an office building or research center, to specific businesses. More fundamentally, book asset values—both before and after accumulated depreciation and amortization—reflect historical cost rather than current value.

The stock price of a successful company will typically exceed book value by a substantial margin, belying any thought that net asset values are representative of economic value. Many companies have business assets (e.g., patents, technical information, established customer base, trained employees, government permits) that do not show up on their balance sheets at all. Also, fixed assets (e.g., land, buildings, and equipment) may be undervalued because of rising replacement costs and the continuing utility of investments that have been partly or fully depreciated.

Using gross assets as the investment denominator is also wrong in principle, because nearly all assets wear out, are depleted, or otherwise lose their economic usefulness over time. On the other hand, gross assets are probably more representative of economic value for many businesses than net assets.

Any given business should be able to establish an appropriate ROI target on an ad hoc basis, but the appropriate target for Business A might seem too high for Business B and not high enough for Business C, depending on such things as their relative capital intensity, stage of life, and competitive situations. Accordingly, buy-in for the ROI system is likely to prove elusive in a company with disparate business units.

Example: DuPont began tracking ROI and component data for its operating divisions in the 1920s, developing a system that would be referred to in the management literature as the "DuPont Method." After the company switched to discounted cash flow measures for investment analyses in the early 1970s, the ROI system began to lose credibility internally.

Among other concerns, ROI was importantly influenced by accounting conventions. Outlays for fixed assets would be capitalized, whereas other types of expenditures that might also create future business value, notably research and development, would be currently expensed and never show up in the investment base. An excessive focus on ROI could therefore have the effect of:

➤ encouraging the acquisition and use of fixed assets through contract manufacture deals or short-term (not capitalized) leases, whether such arrangements were economically advantageous or not

➤ treating research and development and other currently expensed outlays as less onerous than construction expenditures, even though the cash flow effect (aside from timing of the tax deduction benefit) was identical

> *After the Conoco acquisition, a concerted effort was made to develop a new way of calculating ROI that would be equally suitable for the chemicals and petroleum segments of the company. A modified ROI approach using a cash generation numerator was provisionally implemented, but failed to win general acceptance.*

In analyzing business alternatives, there is no substitute for the economic value of assets, i.e., the value realizable from their highest and best use. This can readily be seen for discrete assets, such as a surplus site that would be attractive for a new shopping mall, unused patents that another company might wish to exploit, or obsolete inventory that should be scrapped to obtain the tax deduction benefit. The same point applies in the case of groups of related assets, such as the assets of a business unit.

Using the same concepts of discounted cash flow that were previously discussed for projects, business cash flows can be projected and discounted at the cost of capital in an effort to determine whether economic or shareholder value will be increased. Projected cash flows should be based on the best available strategy and reflect capital expenditures, research and development, or other discretionary spending that would be needed to support the strategy.

The value of continuing to operate the business unit can then be calculated as:

Discounted present value
of future cash flows
minus
Realizable after-tax value
from a current divestiture

If the indicated result is positive and there is a high degree of confidence in future cash flows, economic value is being added and the business should be continued. Otherwise, divestiture of the business (or its constituent parts if the breakup value is greater) may be the best course of action.

Net present value analyses require substantial effort, and the results must be assessed with care because many assumptions are involved. Nevertheless, there is no reason NPV cannot be used periodically in tracking the performance of business units as well as assessing potential transactions.

CEO: What about imposing a capital charge on assets in lieu of NPV?
CFO: Such an approach doesn't avoid the basic problem with ROI, namely that book asset values aren't representative of economic value, but it may be worth doing as a supplement to NPV.

Many companies have imposed a capital charge to impress on business managers that there is a cost involved in financing the assets used in their businesses. Such a charge may be based on current borrowing rates or the cost of capital. Some companies impose the charge on total assets, while others apply it only to working capital on the grounds that this investment is more controllable in the short run.

Imposing a capital charge can achieve quick benefits if business managers have been accustomed to thinking of financial costs as a "corporate problem," and is certainly better than allowing such a mindset to persist. To the extent that the resulting charges differ from the real capital costs of the business (economic value $\times$ cost of capital), however, the long-term effects are problematic.

Even in the short run, charging the cost of capital on working capital can lead to erroneous decisions. Thus, a business might offer early payment discounts to reduce accounts receivable, even though the company's only immediate use for the funds is to pay down borrowings that cost less than the discount. Presumably, the best decision can be made with appropriate guidance from Finance. At least, businesspeople would understand that there is a tradeoff involved and that the cost of financing working capital is attributable to their operations.

CEO: I've got a basic concern about using NPV as a business performance measure, namely how to cope with unrealistic forecasts.

CFO: As with investment proposals, it's essential to test the underlying assumptions for reasonableness.

Say the business is a new venture. An advocate will anticipate success and forecast the financial results accordingly. With an existing business, the traps to watch out for are unsupported departures from historical experience, and the tendency for complacency to set in.

Any NPV analysis should be probed to ensure that foreseeable developments have been reflected, by asking questions such as:

➤ How much are customers willing and able to pay for our products or services, and why? Are customer preferences (e.g., for "hula hoops") likely to change quickly?

➤ What sort of new technology is in the pipeline, either in our company or elsewhere? Are there other technologies, perhaps not quite as good but a lot cheaper (see the Iridium example), that could undercut this business?

➤ Who are the major competitors, either presently or prospectively? What sort of financial results have they achieved? What initiatives might they undertake to capture market share?

➤ Is there exposure to a major change in prices for key materials or services?

➤ Will employees with new skills have to be recruited, and what will they have to be paid? How much expense has been assumed for retraining current employees?

➤ If all the components are purchased from other firms, what assurance can there be that these suppliers will not forward integrate at some point?

History is not necessarily a guide to the future of an established business, but be on the lookout for unsupported departures from previous trends. Say that sales volume for the business has been growing about 1 percent per year, and starting in the second forecast year, the growth rate jumps to 5 percent. Unless there is a solid explanation for this discontinuity, the analysis should be sent back for reworking. Similar tests can be made for cash outlays, especially discretionary expenditures for fixed assets and research and development. Financial ratios such as profit margin and inventory turns, should also be scrutinized.

Ensure that the forecast cases will be retained for future reference. In a year or two, the excessive optimism of an earlier forecast may stick out like a sore thumb.

In short, management should ask the right sort of questions and make clear that it wants realistic answers. The NPV analyses will greatly improve as a result, even though they will continue to fall short of perfection.

Note that every public company has a built-in reality check

for internal NPV analyses, namely the total of its business valuations (discounted present value of future cash flows) should be in synch with its stock price. If there is a big difference, a question must be asked: Who is right, the company or the stock market?

CEO: Suppose one of the businesses is very different from the rest of the company, and deserves a higher multiple because of explosive growth prospects, but the securities analysts just don't see the potential.

CFO: The cleanest answer may be to sell the distinctive business or spin it off as a separate company. Another approach is to issue a tracking stock based on its results as compared with those of the company as a whole.

There was a time when diversification was in vogue, and companies would enter all kinds of businesses as though there was some generic way to run a business that could be applied to everything from coal mining to fish farming.

In recent years, the pendulum has swung back in the direction of concentrating on a specific business or a family of closely related businesses. Most of the acquisitions now are consolidations of players within a given industry, who are taking advantage of the removal of barriers to international competition.

Example: One of the best known so-called conglomerates was created by Harold Geneen, who in 1959 took the reins of International Telephone & Telegraph (ITT), a group of telephone companies with annual sales of about $800 million.

Under Geneen's tireless leadership, ITT acquired approximately 350 companies in a variety of industries and grew to annual sales of over seventeen billion dollars. The portfolio was basically managed by monitoring business unit performance against financial objectives. So long as ITT enjoyed a high stock market multiple and could use its stock to acquire companies selling at a lower price/earnings ratio, everything was rosy.

Eventually this strategy began to falter. On a single day in July 1984, the ITT stock price fell by nearly one-third in reaction to an unexpected dividend cut. Geneen's successor reversed course and sold off some 200 of the businesses that Geneen had acquired. In 1995, the remainder of ITT was split up into three pieces: a financial services company (insurance), an industrial company (automotive, defense, electronics, and fluid technology), and a third company that owned, among other things, hotels.

Geneen remained active after he left ITT, taking a role in other businesses and writing several books about management. His credo remained that, come what may, the essence of managing a business is to meet the financial commitments that have been made.

Among the reasons for the current emphasis on business focus is the perceived investor preference for focused investments. Although diversification can clearly be helpful in reducing investment risk, investors believe they should be able to decide for themselves which industries to reflect in their portfolios rather than relying on the discretion of corporate managers. Also, there are many opportunities for geographical expansion in the global business arena.

If a company has a business that is not related to its other operations, a spin-off will make the company a more focused investment and facilitate evaluation of the divested business on its own merits. If the market places a higher value on the two separate pieces than it did on the combination, the result will be an increase in shareholder value. Generally, a spin-off can be effected as a "tax-free" transaction.

Perhaps the divesting company wants to realize cash from the transaction as opposed to simply separating diverse operations. The company may want to sell the business rather than spinning it off, even though the resulting gain would be taxable.

One variation on the spin-off theme is an initial public offering for the business to be divested to generate some cash, followed by a spin-off of the rest of its stock. Another is a split-off; investors are asked to choose which part of the company they wish to hold. Competent tax advice is essential in planning such transactions, and an advance ruling from the Internal Revenue Service (IRS) is generally advisable.

The tracking stock idea was developed in the 1980s as a means to satisfy the perceived need to distinguish disparate businesses that management did not desire to divest. Thus, General Motors issued "lettered" stocks for its Electronic Data Systems (which was later divested) and Hughes Electronics subsidiaries (which securities analysts are still urging be divested), and USX issued separate stocks for USX-Steel and USX-Marathon (oil) in the context of a contentious dispute with Carl Icahn.

Essentially, a *tracking stock* is a class of shares that conveys a claim to the earnings and assets of a particular business within a company. Holders of such a stock are therefore primarily concerned with the performance and prospects of the specific business, as distinguished from the performance and prospects of the overall company. As a prerequisite, the assets and accounting of the company must be compartmentalized. Now the board will be, in effect, managing different businesses for different groups of shareholders instead of seeking to maximize the value of the total company for all the shareholders.

A number of major companies (e.g., AT&T; Donaldson, Lufkin & Jenrette; DuPont; General Electric; Microsoft; Sprint; and Walt Disney) have recently issued or are considering issuing tracking stocks—generally to highlight the performance of a fast-growing business in the portfolio. Such an approach may arguably contribute to the maximization of shareholder value, but critics claim that shareholders are often unclear as to what assets they actually own. Tracking stock may spawn future litigation by shareholders that claim that a business decision benefited shareholders of another class, while improperly slighting their own interests.

CEO: Suppose the real problem is an overly complacent business culture? Short of encouraging a raider to take over the company, how could a company solve a problem like that with financial thinking?

CFO: Borrow to its financial limit and use the proceeds to re-purchase stock or pay a special dividend. Such a leveraged recapitalization will both reward the stockholders and bring home the cost of capital to the organization in a very tangible way.

Internal complacency typically sets in because a company begins to rely on its past successes. Even if the company is still doing reasonably well, trouble may loom down the road.

Say the company is no longer growing and its internal cash flow is more than adequate to cover all the projects that are indicated for its existing business. If necessary, ample unused borrowing capacity exists to cover a shortfall in any given year.

The employees are well paid and enjoy generous fringe benefits, most of the customers seem satisfied, and there are no apparent problems with suppliers or the government. Everyone is happy except the shareholders, who receive a decent dividend but have seen the market value of the company's stock stagnate.

Since the company has a limited number of high return projects to invest in, perhaps it can invest in its own business by repurchasing stock. The funding can readily be arranged by using its unused borrowing capacity, which costs far less than equity financing. If the transaction is properly conceived, three things should be accomplished:

1. The stock price will perk up, thereby rewarding the long-suffering shareholders. Perhaps a higher stock price will put the company in a better position to grow by acquiring other businesses, or to raise funds when needed by reselling the same number of shares at a much higher price. If a takeover offer comes along instead, the bidding will start at a higher level.

2. There is likely to be a shift in the perceptions of shareholders in connection with a leveraged buyout or recapitalization, resulting in fewer shareholders that are primarily interested in short-term earnings and more that are focused on longer-term cash flow.

3. Financial flexibility for the future will have been utilized. To cover the significantly higher interest expense and start amor-

tizing the added debt, employees at all levels will begin scrutinizing operating and capital expenditures far more closely than they have been accustomed to doing. The effect of such scrutiny is likely to be strongly positive.

> Example: At a time when its stock was selling for $70 per share and there were no takeover offers on the table, FMC Corporation initiated a leveraged recapitalization. Public shareholders were offered $70 in cash (to be borrowed) plus one new share for each of their existing shares. Insiders were offered less cash and more new shares, with the result that their ownership of the company's stock would increase from 19 to 41 percent.
>
> The stock price rose from $70 to nearly $100 after this transaction was announced, and FMC responded by raising the offer for public shareholders to $80 plus one new share. According to Bennett Stewart of Stern Stewart & Co., the value of FMC stock rose for three reasons:
>
> ➤ "Operating profits for the foreseeable future will be sheltered almost entirely from corporate taxation. In effect, FMC became a partnership for tax purposes."
>
> ➤ "With discretionary cash flow dedicated to debt service, the risk of an unproductive investment has been eliminated for some time."
>
> ➤ "Management and employees were given a far greater incentive to perform well and more obvious penalties for failure."
>
> *After the recapitalization, FMC widened its operating profit margins and dramatically improved its working capital management.*[1]

CEO: I thought lenders demanded a substantial equity base. How much debt can a company take on?

CFO: There is a limit, but it's based on future cash flows rather than balance sheet numbers. Finding the limit tends to be a process of trial and error.

Traditionally, it has been suggested that certain balance sheet relationships should be maintained; e.g., the debt ratio [total debt divided by (total debt + stockholders' equity)] should not exceed X percent. (The applicable percentage has been thought to range from say 20 percent for a high technology company to 70 percent for a regulated public utility.) However, the real question is not the book debt ratio, but whether future cash flows will be adequate to provide reasonable assurance that all debt service payments can be covered. The board of directors may decide to issue so much debt and buy back so much stock in a recapitalization that stockholders' equity is reduced to a negative number (as happened in the FMC case).

Even if a leveraged recapitalization is deemed supportable, it will still increase the risk of default to some degree. New lenders will therefore require a higher interest rate, and existing lenders may seek to negotiate the interest rate they are receiving if they have any leverage (e.g., covenants in debt instruments) to do so.

When stockholder's equity is negative, there may be a legal ban on paying dividends. To avoid this constraint as a result of the proposed transaction, the company's independent accountant should be asked whether the assets of the company can be "written up" to current market value.

If several bidders are competing for control of a given company, how much debt is issued may ultimately depend on the judgment of the highest bidder. Deals will be entered into that "push the envelope," just as the ancient Egyptians experienced setbacks in building pyramids before ascertaining the upper limit on the slope of these structures.

> Example: During the 1980s, there was a series of leveraged buyouts in which acquiring groups borrowed against the assets of a target company to raise most of the money to acquire them. Several of these transactions involved billions of dollars, culminating with the acquisition of RJR Nabisco in 1989 (when junk bond financing was beginning to fall out of favor).
>
> RJR Nabisco was placed into play when a manage-

ment-led buyout group offered $75 per share, which was well above the prevailing stock price. Other bidders surfaced, and the action heated up to a fevered pitch. Kohlberg Kravis Roberts & Co. (KKR) eventually won the auction for $109 per share, raising most of the price through debt financing.

After the acquisition, RJR Nabisco experienced initial losses because of vastly increased interest expense, and it implemented some painful cutbacks. Having included a "reset" (restore to face value) provision for bonds issued in the acquisition that were trading at a deep discount, KKR found it necessary to provide a $6.9 billion refinancing package in 1990 to cover the repurchase of the original bonds and the substitution of less onerous forms of debt. [2]

CEO: Given all that we have talked about, why isn't financial thinking breaking out all over without any need for encouragement?

CFO: It takes more than financial thinking to run a business, and other perspectives have been marketed very effectively. Also, any organization pays attention to the ideas that the top management values—whether or not these ideas are right.

Think about all the management gurus and consultants who are trying to peddle their wares to the corporate world. They are not likely to get ahead by preaching the old-time religion, because everyone has already heard it. The trick is to come up with a message that sounds new and is plausible enough to get in the door.

Several of the new ideas that are currently in vogue, put forth by the gurus and consultants, compare with the old thinking (stated first) as follows:

➣ Managers work the business strategy, allocating resources and pushing for incremental gains to enhance the bottom line. Leaders should concentrate on promoting a vision that will energize the organization to shoot for the far horizon.

➤ A company is run to benefit its shareholders. A company should be run for the benefit of all of its stakeholders.

➤ Once employees did what they were told by their boss. Now teams of employees should be empowered to run the business.

➤ Winning is everything. The goal should be win-win solutions.

➤ The old scorecard was a summary of financial data. The new scorecard must include many nonfinancial perspectives.

The new thinking is not totally off base, for the world is a very different place than it was a hundred years ago. It would be fatal to pretend otherwise.

To use Peter Drucker's terminology, our economy and the businesses that make it up have become increasingly "knowledge-based." Proportionately fewer employees are engaged in the production of goods, a form of activity susceptible to being organized along hierarchical lines. Ever more employees are involved in providing services and manipulating mental concepts, a form of output that cannot be effectively supervised from afar.

Some of the middle management layers were needed in the past to aid in the collection and dissemination of information. This need has been greatly reduced by the computerization of business processes and systems, which has made it both feasible and competitively imperative to eliminate some of these layers.

Ever faster change in the business world has placed a premium on rapid decision making, which is hardly the hallmark of a hierarchical organization structured along rigid functional lines.

Consider how much time would be wasted if marketing issues had to be reviewed by an appropriate marketing manager, technical issues had to be reviewed by an appropriate R&D manager, etc., before there was any working-level testing of the decisions with other functions. Things can get done much faster if a marketing person, technical person, financial person, etc., are assigned to work together on a critical task that requires multifunctional expertise. This does not mean the functional managers concerned will not review the resulting plan, but the potential for delay and wasted effort is greatly reduced all the same.

Although there are cogent reasons for the new business thinking, it seems fair to add that the advocates of change tend to exaggerate the importance and novelty of their points.

➤ Win-win solutions are great, but the concept—if not the term—was suggested by Dale Carnegie (author of *How to Win Friends and Influence People*, published in 1938) and others a long time ago.

➤ Even in the old days when businesses were organized in functional stovepipes, employees often found ways to share information and make the system work.

➤ An excessively narrow focus on the bottom line has never been a good business practice, nor is it a news flash that a business that ignores the interests of its customers and employees is headed for trouble.

When all is said and done, financial thinking simply has not been given much recognition in recent management literature. It is old-fashioned, myopic, and above all negative, or so many people believe. These are just perceptions, of course, but they do influence actual behavior.

CEO: Some of the new management thinking is pretty faddish, but what have strategy gurus like Michael Porter been saying?

CFO: Porter emphasizes the logical as opposed to emotional side of management, but gives very little recognition to the importance of financial thinking. In his view, the relevant financial issues are of secondary importance and rather easily addressed. In recent years, other strategic theorists have done no better in this respect.

In a Boston Consulting Group model that was popular in the 1970s, businesses were said to fit into one of four categories: high market share/high growth—stars; low market share/high growth—question marks; high market share/low growth—cows; and low market share/low growth—dogs. The idea was to fund the stars, watch the question marks, milk the cows, and shoot the dogs.

Rejecting this model as simplistic, which it obviously was, Michael Porter developed a sophisticated theory of how a business can seek to achieve sustainable competitive advantage. His approach was presented in *Competitive Strategy* (1980), and elaborated on and extended in *Competitive Advantage* (1985) and *The Competitive Advantage of Nations* (1990).

Porter postulates that there are two basic strategies for a company seeking to build competitive advantage. One is to become the low cost producer. The other is to differentiate its product offering to meet the needs of customers better than anyone else does. Either approach can apply for the market as a whole, or alternatively be pursued within selected niches of the market.

Selecting a strategy is not necessarily a choice, and Porter advocates that the strategist undertake a detailed value chain analysis to identify areas of competitive advantage that a company might have. For purposes of such an analysis, the primary activities of the company are considered to be inbound logistics, operations, outbound logistics, marketing and sales, and service. Procurement, technology development, and human resources are classified as support activities. Everything else, including general management, planning, finance, and accounting, falls into the category of infrastructure, which are costs to be minimized.

A market differentiation strategy seems inherently more interesting than striving to be the low cost producer, if nothing else because it offers a potential escape from the tyranny of cost constraints. As though to encourage such a view, Porter cautions that the worst choice a company can make is to concentrate on both differentiation and cost and get stuck in the middle. One might wonder whether real life businesses can make such an "either/or" choice. [3]

Example: DuPont traditionally stressed the development of exciting new products, and the differentiation of its offering to meet customer requirements. The company's "staff departments" were also first class. Over time, competitors made inroads in many of DuPont's markets, and a message began to come back from long-term customers to the effect that "you are our preferred supplier, your product and service are superb, but we simply can't afford to continue buying from you." The inevitable response was several years of corporate restructuring to achieve a more competitive cost position.

In developing his theories, Porter pays surprisingly little attention to the potential gains from creative financial thinking. In *Competitive Strategy*, there is no substantive mention of the role of Finance. In *Competitive Advantage*, which many consider to be his most important work, he devotes only three pages to Finance in a 557-page book and addresses the area as though it was included only in the interests of completeness. In Porter's own words:

> *There are two basic sources of financial interrelationships: joint raising of capital and shared utilization of capital (primarily working capital). Economies of scale and shared utilization of capital may indeed exist, especially up to a certain quantity of capital needed. Efficient utilization of working capital is made possible by counter cyclical or counter seasonal needs for funds among business units, which allows cash freed up by one business unit to be deployed in another. Financial interrelationships typically involve relatively few compromise costs that must be offset against any savings. Moreover, financial interrelationships are among the easiest to achieve if they are present, perhaps a reason why they are so frequently discussed.*
>
> *The major limitation to the competitive advantage of shared financing is the efficiency of capital markets. Scale economies in financing appear to be moderate for most firms and lead to a relatively small*

difference in financing costs. Firms can also borrow to cover short-term cash needs and lend excess cash in the highly efficient markets for commercial paper and other instruments, mitigating the value of sharing working capital. Hence, financial interrelationships are rarely the basis for creating a significant competitive advantage, unless the size and credit ratings of competitors differ greatly.[4]

So there you have it. According to Porter, financial issues relate to efficiency rather than effectiveness, the solutions are not particularly difficult, and more than enough has been written about them already. Unfortunately, this mindset has influenced the thinking of many businesspeople.

Other business strategy writers have offered an eclectic collection of ideas in recent years, such as driving core competencies, reengineering processes, and reinventing the business by changing the rules of the game. They generally have not had much to say about financial issues, and there has been little discernible elevation of financial thinking on the corporate totem pole.

CEO: What does Peter Drucker have to say about financial thinking?
CFO: Drucker may be the exception that proves the rule. His earlier writings include some insightful commentary about financial issues, even though his far-ranging and provocative comments about major trends in the business world are better known.

In *Managing for Results* (1964), Drucker demonstrates an obvious respect for financial thinking and an appreciation for what is involved. Thus, he:

➢ describes a contemporaneous transactional analysis of business costs by McKinsey & Co. that sounds remarkably like activity-based costing.

➢ observes that "few things are as expensive as the wrong financial structure" and as "completely hidden in the traditional approach to costs."

➤ suggests that one of the most difficult cost issues is waste, because the "costs of not-doing tend to be hidden in the figures."

➤ advocates full disclosure of the risk of business proposals. "No proposal should be seriously considered unless it presents bluntly and without concealment the worst that could conceivably happen."

➤ alludes to a growing recognition of the importance of financial issues. "It is, as a rule, easier to speed up the turnover of money than to do much about unsatisfactory profit margins. Yet only in the last few years have American managements taken seriously the management of money in the business. Indeed, this job has only recently been accepted as an important function of management, for which somebody in the top group has to be responsible, and on which somebody has to work full time."[5]

Well said! Clearly here is someone who could have been a fine financial executive if such had been his desire. Instead, Drucker was fascinated with analyzing the big picture, and became a management visionary whose published work is remarkable for its scope and diversity.

CEO: You have made some excellent points about the power of financial thinking, but how can we drive this kind of thinking through the organization?

CFO: I believe we can get there by encouraging everyone in Finance to act as shareholder value enablers.

CEO: I thought you would suggest a smaller nucleus, such as the financial planning group, but by all means let's talk this thing through.

SUMMING UP

➤ Better financial thinking is a mindset for finding the most productive ways to cope with the reality that all organizations must compete for resources on a continuing basis. This mindset provides true competitive advantage and creates shareholder value.

➤ Book revenue, cost, and asset data are not adequate for business decision making, which requires a focus on the future rather than the past.

➤ In principle, an NPV analysis based on projected cash flows is the best approach to assessing whether a business is earning the cost of capital, but the underlying assumptions must be closely scrutinized.

➤ A wide range of issues can be addressed with financial thinking, from determining the appropriate capital structure to assessing restructuring opportunities. It can help to unlock hidden value in the corporate portfolio (e.g., spin-off), or to shake up a complacent business culture (leveraged recapitalization).

➤ Most of the leading management theorists underestimate the power of financial thinking, and their ideas have influenced the perceptions of many businesspeople.

NOTES

1. G. Bennett Stewart, III, *The Quest for Value: A Guide for Senior Managers* (New York: HarperBusiness/HarperCollins Publishers, 1991), 557–565. Copyright © 1990 by Ballinger Company. Reprinted by permission of HarperCollins Publishers, Inc.
2. Bryan Burrough and John Helyar, *Barbarians at the Gate: The Fall of RJR Nabisco* (New York: HarperPerennial/HarperCollins Publishers, 1991). Copyright © 1990 by Bryan Burrough and John Helyar. Reprinted by permission of HarperCollins Publishers, Inc.
3. Joseph H. Boyett and Jimmie T. Boyett, *The Guru Guide: The Best Ideas of the Top Management Thinkers* (New York: John Wiley & Sons, 1998), 175–192. © 1998 Joseph H. Boyett and Jimmie T. Boyett.
4. Michael E. Porter, *Competitive Advantage: Creating and Sustaining Superior Performance* (New York: The Free Press, 1985), 348–349.

© 1985, 1998 by Michael E. Porter. Reprinted with permission of The Free Press, a Division of Simon & Schuster.

5. Peter F. Drucker, *The Executive in Action* (from *Managing for Results*, 1964), (New York: HarperBusiness/HarperCollins Publishers, 1996), 46–48, 86, 87, 100, 232. Copyright © 1964 by Peter F. Drucker. Reprinted by permission of HarperCollins Publishers, Inc.

Chapter Four

THE FINANCE OF TODAY AND TOMORROW

The difficult we do immediately. The impossible takes a little longer.

U.S. Army Service Forces, 1940s

CEO: I'm sure you've got a lot of ideas about turning your people into shareholder value enablers, but let's start at the beginning. What can you tell me about Finance, and what it has to offer?

CFO: Every activity in the company is intertwined with financial results. Someone has to handle the money and keep score. Traditionally, that's been the role of Finance. It gives us an appreciation of the need to drive shareholder value, and a leg up in spotting opportunities to do so.

Finance is a network that consists of people in the central Finance organization, affiliated personnel located within the businesses, and external partners, such as the independent accountants, investment and commercial bankers, tax counsel, actuaries, and financial service firms.

The CFO is responsible for the activities of all three categories of people. Contracting out a financial function may reduce a company's headcount, and possibly its costs, but will not shift the responsibility for ensuring that the function is being performed effectively.

Aside from the common denominator of the activities, which is money, there is an enormous diversity in Finance activities. The following discussion might be typical for a large company that has not made much use of outsourcing:

➤ Treasury borrows money and manages a company's cash. The effort is centralized for maximum efficiency, e.g., funds will not be borrowed to meet the needs of Business A if they are available from Business B. Treasury also handles foreign exchange transactions and hedging, administers the company's insurance and risk management program, develops and administers customer financing programs, etc.

➤ Investor relations handles inquiries from the investment community, and tries to put news about company activities in the most positive light (which includes acknowledging unfavorable developments when applicable, rather than trying to push them under the carpet).

➤ Financial planning and analysis coordinates the company's budgeting process, reviews the financial aspects of business plans and investment proposals, and serves as a center of excellence on financial techniques. If there is an acquisition, divestiture, or joint venture under consideration, it will handle the financial review and/or coordinate with the external financial advisor, as well as with the businesspeople.

At least part of the financial planning and analysis activity is decentralized, so as to get closer to the businesses where many of the key decisions are being made. The financial analysts concerned would typically report to someone in the business, but receive functional guidance from the corporate Finance organization.

➤ Corporate accounting prepares the financial statements that are published externally. It is responsible for complying with the complex and at times confusing requirements of the Financial Accounting Standards Board (FASB) and other standard-setting groups. Corporate accounting also generates the internal financial statements that management uses in running the company and businesses and provides related analyses. The information for the company's financial statements typically flows in from satellite accounting systems operated by domestic and international subsidiaries and affiliates. Cost accounting systems tend to be even more decentralized, and may be located at the business or unit level.

➤ The tax department prepares and defends returns for all the jurisdictions in which the company operates. In the case of income tax returns, the published financial statements are the starting point, but many adjustments are required to get the numbers on a tax wavelength. Another critical role for the tax staff is to provide guidance on the tax implications of proposed business transactions. Sometimes the treatment of a given item will seem surprising, but as the saying goes, "Who says the tax law has to be logical?"

➤ Credit works with the businesses in evaluating the creditworthiness of potential customers and setting payment terms. It then follows up with customers who are late in paying their bills, seeking to hold accounts receivable within planned levels. A relatively low level of credit losses is typically a good sign, but a complete absence of such losses may indicate that the credit area is being managed with undue conservatism resulting in lost sales.

➤ Accounts receivable is the custodian of records of amounts due from customers and others. In addition to questions about the accuracy of billings, it fields many inquiries relating to product or service quality. A failure to address such concerns promptly can not only result in late payment, but also impede the flow of new orders.

➤ Accounts payable performs the reverse function, receiving bills from external parties, appropriately verifying that they are in order, and arranging for payment. Much of the company's cash outlays pass through this area, creating the potential for costly mistakes. Thus, management may not even be aware of the money being lost if accounts payable is failing to take advantage of early payment discounts. In addition, accounts payable reimburses employees for travel expense.

➤ Payrolls and employee benefits see to it that salaries and wages are paid and that employees receive the benefits that are provided for in the company benefit plans. No error is more certain to be noticed than a paycheck that is late or incorrect.

➤ Auditing tries to confirm that company policies and procedures are being followed by monitoring business and financial transactions for compliance therewith. Few things can be as embarrassing to a company as to learn that earnings have been misstated or that a major fraud has been committed. The independent accountant's review of the annual financial statements provides limited protection in this regard.

➤ Information technology may be a part of Finance or exist as a separate operation. Either way, Finance has a vital responsibility in ensuring the integrity, usefulness, and cost effectiveness of the computer programs and records that comprise the bulk of the company's financial information system.

CEO: I've met many of the people in treasury, investor relations, financial planning, accounting, and tax. The other groups are pretty much an unknown to me, and I'm wondering whether they don't simply represent overhead that should be reduced as much as possible and then reduced some more.

CFO: That's the indicated answer so long as these groups are viewed as merely providing services for "internal customers." I believe they could do far more, and that with all the streamlining that has taken place, the focus should now be on unlocking their potential to add value.

In principle, overhead represents costs for activities that are needed by the total company, but are unnecessary for its constituent businesses. Only a few corporate activities represent overhead in this sense, although businesspeople often apply the label indiscriminately.

Example: A few years ago, Finance at DuPont conducted a major study of "overhead activities" because business managers were critical of the costs of such activities. The study showed that at least 90 percent of the corporate activities in question were required by the businesses, e.g., paying employees and suppliers, collecting receivables, initiating and defending lawsuits, filing patent applications, negotiating labor contracts, administering benefit plans, and so on. The much smaller segment of activities required only by corporate included such activities as investor and shareholder relations and maintaining contacts with the media.

With respect to the 90 percent that turned out to be "business" activities rather than "overhead" activities, the businesses were given the freedom to purchase such "business" activities outside the company if they wished. Hardly anyone did this, and the criticism of "overhead activities" died down noticeably.

Like other areas, Finance in most companies has seen its share of restructuring and cost reduction.

➤ Task teams met to discuss how activities could be reengineered to cut out unnecessary steps, which in effect redesigned processes from the ground up.

➤ In conjunction with an outside consultant, benchmarking studies were undertaken to compare internal processes to comparable processes at companies who reportedly had achieved "the best of the best" status in a particular area.

➤ Early retirement offers were extended, with particular emphasis on thinning the ranks of middle management.

When the dust settled, essential functions were still getting done. There were a few glitches, but no major disasters.

Using the logic previously discussed regarding the limits of debt financing (see Chapter 3), a company could choose to continue reducing the resources for staff functions until something fundamental started to crack.

Certain activities should be exempted. The value of an innovative financing technique, insightful financial study, or creative tax idea can be tremendous. No need to kill the goose capable of laying golden eggs. Accounting might also qualify, given that corporate management must sign off on the financial statements.

The payoffs in other areas are less obvious, and may tend to be taken for granted. That is where Finance has the most work to do in terms of enhancing the value of its services and obtaining the appropriate recognition.

Take auditing, for instance. As long as the focus is limited to catching fraud and such, the group can never expect to be very popular. One idea for improvement is to conduct operational audits and offer cost-saving and revenue-enhancement ideas along with findings regarding compliance issues. Even if 75 percent of such ideas prove impracticable, a few hits should convince the businesspeople that the auditors are playing on the same team. Viewing operations from a business perspective could also be an antidote for tunnel vision.

Example: After DuPont's Brazilian subsidiary acquired a small fabricator of engineering polymer parts, the manager was told that the operating results had to be improved. The business subsequently began to report profits, but inventories soared. Auditing determined that the pounds of polymer on hand agreed precisely with the inventory records, but failed to note that defective parts were being carried in inventory at manufacturing cost instead of scrap value. By the time this problem was detected, an unanticipated write-off was required.

Accounts receivable is in direct contact with the company's customers, who provide the revenues (inflow of cash) to keep the company in business. When customers call with billing inquiries, there is no good reason why they should have to spend five minutes navigating through a voice mail system, only to be told that all the company's representatives are busy. The background music and statements that "your call is very important to us" do not greatly improve the situation. Perhaps the company could gain a competitive advantage by taking the opposite tack, and providing better service.

Example: At Nortel Networks, a European accounting manager invited two Finance executives from a large European customer to accompany him to North America for two weeks where he could show them Nortel's management accounting systems. He then assisted them in developing their finance systems strategies after they returned to Europe. This initiative was much appreciated by the customer, and more than paid for itself.

Another idea for accounts receivable is to create a systematic record of customer complaints. Such a database is potentially more informative and less costly than marketing surveys of people who may not even be customers or know anything about the product. Also, there is no good reason why someone with a gripe should have to write corporate management or post a note on an Internet bulletin board before anyone starts paying attention.

Accounts payable is a group that is not easy to glamorize, but it handles much of the company's disbursements and that adds up to big bucks. This group must arrange for timely payment of all of the bills that are in order (taking all available discounts), and ensure that other bills are identified and held up until open issues can be resolved. It might be necessary to withhold payment for such things as nonconforming product or services, pricing errors, or even invoices submitted fraudulently. Everyone that accounts payable comes in contact with should be treated professionally; voice mail systems can be just as irritating for the company's valued suppliers as for its customers.

Accounts payable should look to the internal group that ordered the product or service in the first place to verify that the value bargained for has been provided. Nevertheless, the procedures required to ensure the appropriate handling of incoming bills are more complex than is commonly realized.

Example: Corning centralized a number of financial services groups in what was called the Administrative Center, instituted team style operations, and improved the professionalism of operations in general.

In accounts payable, the traditional system of assigning people to individual functions (data entry, calculation of cash discount, checking for systems authorization, etc.) was replaced by a system in which the assigned payables representative did the entire job for a particular group of suppliers. As a result, this person was in a position to answer questions without having to go to the other desks or the correspondence files for information.[1]

The discussion goes on to credit, payrolls, and other groups. In each case, the challenge is to find ways to enhance the group's contribution and make it more apparent to others within the company.

CEO: I recognize that many of the Finance people are dealing with our customers and suppliers, and that they may come across information of value to the businesses. Still, the kind of contributions that the back office groups can make wouldn't really drive better financial thinking in this company. What do you think could do the trick?

CFO: I don't believe we can afford to neglect the "back office" groups, as you call them, if nothing else because impressions of the various groups tend to blend together. So long as certain Finance groups have a bad reputation, whether deservedly or otherwise, this will color the perceptions of everyone else.

The "front office" groups also need to demonstrate that they can bring value to the businesses. One key project would be to upgrade the budgeting process.

CEO: Now there's a good idea. Tell me more.

CFO: Budgeting will always involve some tension, given the issues at stake, such as which businesses are "stars" and which are "cows." We should be able to reduce the level of nonproductive posturing, however, by integrating the several phases of the process with an NPV focus.

Traditionally, the budget review has been conducted in several different stages that are only loosely linked together, namely:

➤ *Earnings budget.* The businesses strive to minimize earnings expectations for the coming year, because it is the principal figure for which they expect to be held accountable in the sense that a shortfall will affect their incentive compensation, performance appraisal, etc. Meanwhile, Finance, with corporate management support, lobbies for more ambitious targets by adding up the business inputs and proclaiming that the total is too low. Projected earnings in the "out years" typically soar, reflecting a perception that no one will ever follow up to see if they are attained. Ever hear of a "hockey stick" forecast?

➤ *Resource budgets.* Budgets are developed separately for headcount, capital expenditures, research and development, advertising, etc. The operative assumption is that there is just so much the company wants or can afford to spend in total, and that this amount needs to be divided among the businesses. The earnings budget dialogue is essentially reversed, with the businesses now attempting to justify high resource support while Finance argues for lower figures.

➤ *Cash flow budget.* Data from the earnings budget and the resource budget reviews are combined with expense budgets for staff groups, interest expenses, etc., to develop the cash flow projections used in assessing financing needs and dividend planning. This is basically a Finance exercise, with the businesses playing a peripheral role.

It can literally take months to complete the annual budget cycle, primarily because the earnings budgets are built up through an iterative process that starts at the grassroots level. Before the annual budget cycle is over, people throughout the company will be muttering that "I wish someone had told me in the first place what the number was supposed to be."

Some of the assumptions that are cranked into the budgeting process at the beginning will be outdated by the time the budget is wrapped up. In terms of accuracy, business managers and Finance might do as well to develop the budget numbers in the course of an afternoon. With such a top down approach, however, most of the employees would be cut out of the loop and have little reason to identify with the resulting targets.

Some have suggested that the answer might be to budget without numbers and without hindsight judgment. In effect, that is what's done at many small businesses where the founder and chief mover is close enough to all of the input and output activities in the business to dispense with a formal set of financial targets.

> Example: Communications Development Co. is a graphic-design business in southwestern Pennsylvania that creates catchy business cards, sets up Web pages, and develops ad campaigns. Initially the company's financial plan was simple: make payroll, keep the lights on. Now with 8 staff members and 120 clients, it is getting hard to be sure which of the projects being worked on are profitable. "We need a budget," concedes cofounder Toby Fancher, but adds that with revenue of some $500,000 per year the company is hardly in the big leagues yet.[2]

In a larger organization, where the efforts of many people contribute to overall results in a manner that can be far from obvious, budgeting without numbers could remove accountability from the system and be a recipe for disaster. So, yes, a budgeting process is needed and the challenge is to obtain more meaningful output, in less time, with a minimum of nonproductive side effects.

The initial step is easy; wring any obvious waste out of the process. Just because computers can handle huge amounts of data does not mean that the human beings who input and use the data have a similar facility. Eliminate some of those meaningless digits in forecast data, going from dollars to thousands of dollars or from thousands to millions. With fewer numbers on the page, the information that is shown will be easier to understand.

Now integrate the three budgets to produce projected business cash flows for the NPV reviews, and some good things will happen:

1. There will be less incentive for the business to minimize short-term expectations while exaggerating longer-term results because the cash flows for every year in the forecast period will be encompassed in the NPV result. There will still be a role for Finance, however, in probing the forecast assumptions.

2. The enthusiasm of the businesses for seeking maximum resource budgets will hopefully be tempered because the resulting expenditures will immediately and fully impact their projected cash flows. Under the traditional approach, capital expenditures in the first year of the forecast have little or no drag effect on the first year's earnings budget because they are not yet being depreciated.

3. Cash flow projections will be perceived as belonging to the businesses rather than as strictly a Finance exercise. If that sparks new interest in more accurately classifying disbursements by business with some help from accounts payable, so much the better.

Another advantage of the NPV approach is that it should spark more thinking about business alternatives. Projected cash flows are supposed to be based on the best business strategy, but this strategy cannot readily be identified without running alternative scenarios based on differing business approaches and levels of resource support. Perhaps several of these scenarios will be presented in the review with corporate management, rather than focusing the entire review on a single case.

CEO: What's the answer to the inefficiency of working from the bottom up to develop performance targets?

CFO: There's no way to completely eliminate that concern without resorting to a top-down budget process, but business leaders should have more dialogue with their people at the outset as to the level of performance expected.

If performance targets and resource budgets are set at the top, the people who must achieve them will not necessarily be motivated to do so. Also, there will be no immediate check on management expectations, which may or may not be realistic. Whatever the pitfalls of establishing targets with a bottom-up process, it would be a mistake to discard this feature of the current budgeting procedures.

It does not follow, however, that the various areas of the organization should be asked to develop performance targets without guidance. If the business managers get together with their people for a preliminary dialogue, a better set of financial objectives should emerge with far less back and forth when the bottom-up budgets are prepared. This discussion should cover factors in the external environment that are expected to impact the company and business, such as economic outlook, competitive situation, and social concerns (e.g., environmental). It also provides an opportunity to informally exchange ideas about the revenue target, and the resources, outlays, and working capital required to support it.

Finally, do not send out the input forms too early. If this is done, some of the information submitted will inevitably become stale and need to be updated before the budget cycle is over.

CEO: I think you could have a winner with budgeting reform. What other ideas do you have to add value?

CFO: Given that timely and insightful information can represent a competitive advantage, accounting is working to speed up the company's financial reports and implement a virtual closing process.

The sooner the businesspeople receive the financial information they need, the faster they will be able to use it to make better decisions. For instance, assume that marketing expense as a percentage of sales is running at an unacceptable level in January. If the businesspeople become aware of this fact early in February, there will be plenty of time to make adjustments and get back on target for the quarter. Such a correction may be far more difficult if this information is not made available until the end of February.

One way to speed up financial reporting is to overhaul the closing process with the objective of reducing the number of steps, reducing unnecessary effort and overtime, and eliminating errors that slow the process down. Another is to streamline the financial reports, e.g., eliminate information that is not truly useful, and round numbers to thousands or millions.

Oddly enough, there is also much to be said for reducing the frequency of reporting. A quarterly rather than monthly closing of the books will save significant effort for accounting personnel, and should generally suffice for external reporting purposes. In the interim, the focus should be on providing the key information that is needed for business decisions. Such information will vary depending on the nature of the business. For example, marketing expenses may be critical for a consumer products business but of minor importance for an electric power company. Moreover, it may well be needed weekly or even daily instead of monthly. A process to provide financial information as and when it is needed, without closing the books, is otherwise known as a "soft" or "virtual" close.

CEO: Sounds good to me, so long as the businesspeople are in agreement.

CFO: They'll be fully consulted. Next, I'd like to talk about some interesting ideas that Treasury has for using what they call financial engineering to help address strategic business issues. The basic concept is to facilitate business transactions by selectively hedging or assuming business risks that other parties aren't comfortable with, and thereby be able to undertake transactions that would be impracticable otherwise. It's essential, of course, that the terms of the transaction be set to fully compensate our company for the risks assumed.

The world is a highly uncertain place, and it is impossible to pursue the opportunities that are available without also incurring risks. An individual or company's degree of comfort with risk will depend on a variety of factors, some relating to the risk and others to the circumstances of the evaluator.

Avoidance of risk is neither ignoble nor cowardly, and people habitually do it every day. Look both ways before you cross the street, back up your computer output, put aside some money for a rainy day, and buckle your seatbelt.

Objectively speaking, there are two good reasons to take a risk. One is that there is a potential reward, so that even though a loss is possible, the "expected outcome" is positive on a probability-weighted basis. Thus, one might bet a dollar on the flip of a coin if the payoff for winning was three dollars. The other is that the risk is either so minor or so remote that it is not worth worrying about.

On the subjective side of the ledger, there is a special reluctance to assume a risk if the results of losing would be disastrous. Few people would want to wager ten million dollars on a coin flip for a thirty million dollar payoff because, unlike the previous case, a loss could not easily be absorbed.

A big company might take such a bet, assuming it was legal, because it has greater financial resources. Indeed, the ability to take big risks is one of the few clear-cut advantages that a big company has over the smaller and often nimbler companies that are emerging as an increasingly important factor in the global economy.

On the other hand, big companies are likely to find it harder to continue growing than small companies, and may be envied and attacked as a result of their very size and power.

Example: One of the world's most successful and richest companies is Microsoft, the developer of the "Windows" suites of computer software and many other innovative products. Along the way, Microsoft acquired a reputation as a ferocious competitor. The Justice Department and a number of state attorneys general reacted to complaints from Microsoft's competitors by bringing a massive anti-trust action.

After a long and bruising proceeding, the trial judge

ruled that Microsoft had acted to monopolize its market. The tone of the factual findings were strong enough to fuel government demands that the company be broken up, although another possible scenario is some sort of negotiated settlement.

Another consideration is the perceived reliability of probability assessments. The odds on a coin flip are well known, but in less familiar situations it may be desirable to run some preliminary tests before placing one's main bet.

All else being equal, human beings are relatively comfortable with risks that are familiar in situations where they have some ability to influence the outcome, and they are less comfortable with unfamiliar or generalized risks that they cannot hope to control. Thus, some people may think they are safer taking a trip in their own automobile, even though flying in a commercial aircraft is, statistically speaking, much safer.

Organizations exhibit similar attitudes. Thus, exposure to wear and tear of physical assets during routine operations are accepted as a matter of course, but most companies would prefer to avoid the risk of losses from fire, storms, etc. A U.S. company may confidently extend credit to customers in Country X, just as it does with domestic customers, but be concerned about exchange rate exposure on the resulting local currency receivables.

Various procedures have been developed to lay off or hedge risks that one would prefer not to assume. For instance, most companies insure property losses from fire or other casualty above specified limits and willingly pay a premium to transfer the risk to an insurance company.

A U.S. company might be able to swap its local currency receivables with Country X companies that have dollars, but it would probably be more convenient to hedge the company's net position (assets minus liabilities) in that currency with forward exchange contracts. Companies that consume basic raw materials such as oil or metals can hedge against purchase price fluctuation in the commodities markets.

Hedging risk is a mixed benefit. The cost will typically take the form of a payment for coverage, forfeiture of upside potential (the Country X currency may appreciate against the dollar, rather than depreciate as feared), or a combination thereof. Such costs must be weighed against the anticipated benefit of the coverage. Thus, a company might well decide at some point to increase its deductible (or level of self-insurance) for casualty losses to reduce insurance premiums.

The hedging of risk as described thus far is basically a Finance exercise, which can be highly sophisticated in application. Here is a description of Merck's approach to hedging foreign currency exposure from the *Financial Executive*.[3]

> *[CFO Judy Lewent's] idea of plain vanilla includes complicated multi-currency basket options whose price depends on volatilities and correlations of all the currencies in the basket, and other financial engineering inventions that look plain only to quants [sic] comfortable with long equations full of Greek letters.*

It is possible to take the financial engineering concept a step further, by viewing the redistribution of risk as a tool for developing tailor-made solutions to strategic business problems. Imagine a proposed transaction that parties A and B wish to undertake. Only one obstacle remains: a risk associated with the transaction that A is unwilling to accept. No standard option or forward contract is available in the financial markets that A could purchase to hedge the risk. Is there another option?

Perhaps B (or someone known to B) would be more willing to assume the risk than A is, based on either a different view of the probabilities or some of the subjective considerations that have been discussed. If so, B might be willing to contractually assume some or all of the risk from A for an agreed quid pro quo, and thereby clear the way to close the deal.

The potential result is a transaction of benefit to both A and B, rather than a failed proposal. Through financial engineering, B may have gained an edge over competitors who had not thought of the approach.

Here are some applications of financial engineering:

> Use purchase contracts (at the buyer's option) to take on more customers without having to invest in peak-period production capacity
> Give customers fixed, variable, and indexed product-pricing alternatives
> Encourage employees to participate in employee stock ownership plans by capping their capital gains in return for a floor on their capital losses.[4]

Several caveats are in order. Financial engineering merely redistributes risk, rather than eliminating it, and the details of such arrangements tend to be complex. Anticipated benefits may not be achieved if some important element of the business situation has been overlooked. The other party may claim that they cannot or should not have to take a loss and they may seek legal redress.

Example: In 1994, Procter & Gamble and Gibson Greetings announced significant losses on interest-rate derivatives they had purchased from Bankers Trust. Both companies claimed that the downside risks of these instruments had not been properly explained. The bank's position was that these sophisticated investors should have known what they were doing ; they just happened to guess wrong as to the direction of interest rates. The disputes were settled out of court.

Long-term residual costs may also result from using financial engineering to secure a one-time benefit.

Example: To facilitate a merger of Delmarva Power & Light Company and Atlantic City Electric Company (ACEC), with the combined company changing its name to Conectiv, a class of common stock (Conectiv A) was created. Conectiv A's claim to dividends, was tied to the ongoing results of the Atlantic City Electric Company operations as opposed to the combined Conectiv results. The ACEC shareholders received a combination of regular Conectiv shares and Conectiv A shares in the merger.

The existence of the Conectiv A shares (representing less than 10 percent of the total market value of Conectiv's common stock) requires an ongoing effort to segregate the results of Conectiv's operations along regional lines, rather than the business sector lines that are typical with tracking stock, maintain two dividend rates, assess the legal implications of business decisions with a regional impact, and provide appropriate information to two groups of stockholders.

CEO: It's interesting how business opportunities can be created by differing perceptions about the exact same risk. Still, there's something to be said for straightforward transactions, in which everyone is clear as to what they are getting.

Aside from reforming the budget process and risk assessments, what else is new in the financial planning area?

CFO: We're working on several other ideas to help the businesses, notably having the financial analysts assigned to them assume primary responsibility for competitive analyses.

There is a natural tendency in any organization to focus on what is happening internally, which is a comfortable approach because internal information is easy to obtain, and internal events seem relatively controllable. Some say, for example, that many of our Federal government leaders spend too much of their time "inside the beltway" talking to each other. External developments may have a far greater impact on how the organization will fare, but they tend to be given short shrift, because it is much harder to unearth the relevant information, let alone influence what is happening.

Clearly, there would be little purpose in spending months polishing the business strategy, only to learn that a competitor had developed a new approach that rendered it obsolete. To avoid such situations, someone in each business needs to keep tabs on competitors using all the information that is legitimately available.

Financial analysts assigned to the businesses are well qualified for this task. They develop an understanding of the industry in carrying out their business role, and, as a result of their Finance experience, they are accustomed to working with an external focus. They are also adept in working with financial data, which should help them to develop better assessments of the financial considerations that will drive the strategies of competitors.

CEO: What else would you like to take over?

CFO: Marketing people are keen on customer value chain analyses, but the results they come up with are often pretty loose. Despite the obvious difficulties, I believe it would be possible for financial analysts to more precisely quantify the profits being earned at each stage, by our suppliers, ourselves, our customers, and the end user.

There was some experimentation with vertical integration by Henry Ford (among others), but most products result from a multi-stage process involving entities that are not under common control. Thus, A owns the iron mine, B makes the steel, C fabricates the steel into auto parts, D assembles automobiles, and E sells automobiles to customers.

The relationship of these parties is cooperative, in the sense that the efforts of all are necessary to put the automobile into the buyer's hands. It is also competitive, as each party is seeking to earn as much as possible of the total profit. A value chain analysis may give one of the participants a better idea of how much of the total profit it is currently earning and help it identify strategies to acquire a bigger share.

As with any model intended to test the effect of business alternatives before they are implemented in the real world, the value chain approach has some weaknesses:

➤ A company may be involved in numerous value chains, in which case an analysis that fully accounted for its purchases and sales might cover a substantial portion of the global economy.

➤ To some degree the beginning or ending point of a value chain is arbitrary. In the automotive supply chain, for instance, automobiles may be acquired by companies and used as a business asset in addition to being sold to consumers.

➤ The value chain model may not be particularly useful for the technology and services industries that represent a rapidly growing share of total economic output. Although there are value chains in such industries, the stages involved are probably less standardized and less stable than in the traditional manufacturing industries.

If the inputs to a value chain analysis are inaccurate or incomplete, it is quite possible that the results will be useless or even misleading.

CEO: Value chain analyses can provide some useful qualitative insights, but I don't see much point in trying to calculate rigorous results using soft data.

More importantly, where is this discussion headed?

CFO: What do you mean?

CEO: What's the basic objective here, or in the modern lingo, what's the vision that you're trying to articulate?

CFO: For all the things that Finance can contribute, we still aren't being routinely involved when the important business decisions are made. Sure, we do our share in the implementation stage, but by then it may be too late for us to add much value.

In short, my vision for Finance is a seat at the decision-making table.

It is time to build a new legacy for Finance, by complementing the traditional emphasis on financial efficiency with a new or rediscovered emphasis on driving capital effectiveness. To do this, it will be necessary for all areas of Finance to continually focus on the capital resources tied up in the businesses and whether such resources are, or are not, being productively employed.

Many tools can be employed in influencing business behaviors toward value-enhancing directions, from optimizing the company's capital structure, divesting peripheral businesses or assets, and making acquisitions that will strengthen a company's position in core businesses, to creating a more value-adding role for accounts payable *et al.*

Finance needs to develop new skills, such as a better understanding of customer needs and the strengths and weaknesses of competitors. One way to accomplish these ends, and add value as well, is to take a more active role in competitive intelligence studies and value-chain analyses.

Finance can also help to differentiate the company from the competition by looking for opportunities to use financial engineering as a strategic tool.

Financial thinking needs to be appreciated by everyone in the organization, but Finance people must provide continuing support. The world is far too complex and fast moving to analyze every conceivable alternative in an even moderately complicated situation, such as the product loss situation that was reviewed in Chapter 3. Whether by training, by skill, or by instinct, Finance people have a knack for identifying the two or three most promising answers to a complex financial issue as well as spotting potential tax planning opportunities, alternative financing programs, etc.

Additional study will probably be needed to confirm the initial framing of the issue and determine the best solution, but the thinking that takes place up front often represents the most important aspect of the Finance contribution. Clearly there is little point in halfway measures, such as having Finance "run the numbers" after a strategic decision has been made.

With a new shareholder value enabling mindset and culture, reinforced by new behaviors and practices, Finance can provide a powerful competitive edge for the company. To achieve this potential, Finance must be an integral member of the business team.

CEO: The Finance vision may need to be tweaked a bit, but the biggest issue is how you're going to get there. We're out of time for today, but I'll have a few suggestions next time.

CFO: Good, because in all honesty I'm stumped. A shareholder value enabling role for Finance seems like a natural, but the response of the business managers to date hasn't exactly been overwhelming.

SUMMING UP

➤ Finance is a network of people engaged in a variety of activities, some having a relatively high profile such as treasury, financial planning, and acquisitions and others involving a high volume of "routine" transactions like collecting receivables and paying bills.

➤ There is a tendency to view Finance (with the possible exception of high-profile groups) as a source of overhead that should be continually reduced.

➤ Finance should shift the focus from cost cutting to adding value, using whatever means are available for each group to upgrade its contribution and reputation as shareholder value enablers.

➤ One initiative with widespread appeal is the development of an integrated and more effective budgeting process. Other thrusts might include shifting risk to facilitate business transactions, sometimes called financial engineering, increasing Finance involvement in competitive reports and customer value chain analyses.

➤ To achieve the full potential of its new shareholder value enabler role, Finance needs to participate in making, as well as implementing, strategic business decisions.

NOTES

1. Henry A. Davis and Frederick C. Militello, *The Empowered Organization: Redefining the Roles and Practices of Finance* (Morristown,

New Jersey: Financial Executives Research Foundation, 1994), 76–78. Reprinted with permission from Financial Executives Research Foundation, Inc.

2. Dan Morse, "Many Small Businesses Don't Devote Time to Planning," *Wall Street Journal,* 7 September 1999.

3. Gregory J. Millman, "Visionary CFOs: Who Are They and How Can You Become One?" *Financial Executive*, January/February 1999, 24.

4. Peter Turfano, "How Financial Engineering Can Advance Corporate Strategy," *Harvard Business Review,* January–February 1996, 136–46.

Chapter Five

THE FINANCE-
AVOIDANCE CULTURE

One says a lot in vain, refusing; The other mainly hears
the "No."

Johann Wolfgang von Goethe, 1787

CEO: So far you've been doing most of the talking in these sessions,
which suits me fine, but I would like to comment on your marketing approach. In my opinion, it could stand some improvement.
CFO: No problem, I need all the help that I can get in that area.
CEO: The starting point is how Finance is currently perceived, which
is something of a mixed bag. Despite a grudging recognition of
technical competence, there is a perception that Finance doesn't
really understand or care what the businesses are all about.

There is an old joke that illustrates how Finance is perceived. A
pilot ran out of gas and landed in a cornfield in the middle of
nowhere. Stumbling out of the plane, he had no idea of his location. How was he going to determine the distance to the nearest
airport where he might obtain help?

Much to the pilot's relief, a local resident ambled up to see
what had happened. "Where am I?" asked the pilot. "You are
200 yards from my house," said the local resident. Obviously, the

resident must have been from Finance, because the information he provided was 100 percent accurate but absolutely irrelevant.

Hopefully, no one really looks at Finance people in such a light, but the story is not totally off the mark in terms of real-world perceptions. For a variety of reasons, many businesspeople tend to avoid Finance whenever possible on the assumption that Finance's input will be of either little or no value.

In other words, there is a Finance-avoidance culture at work. Finance may still have some clout in such a culture, but it will typically be based—at least initially—on the perceived support of top management.

> Example: Nortel Networks often selected business managers to head Finance, treating these rotational assignments as a developmental move for the individuals concerned. For this and other reasons, Finance had played a somewhat secondary role in the company.
>
> The new CEO, Paul Stern, believed that a different approach was needed, and brought in a CFO with a mandate to professionalize and centralize the function. The level of Finance involvement in strategic business decisions soared after the CEO deferred action on just a couple of major proposals by the subsidiary presidents until the CFO's input had been obtained.

A sense of history may be helpful to understand the prevalence of a Finance-avoidance culture, because many of the current perceptions stem from the practices, terminology, and symbols of yesteryear. Here are a few of the highlights:

➤ The world's oldest surviving written documents are almost exclusively of a business or administrative character, e.g., inventory and tax collection records. Apparently, the ancient Sumerians did not have a very effective "records destruction" program.

➤ "Double entry bookkeeping" was developed in Italy about 500 years ago, and greatly facilitated the emerging concept of business firms with an identity separate from that of the family owners. In addition, as is more commonly remembered, this procedure provided a useful check on clerical errors.

➤ The origin of the term "bean counter" is obscure, but it may well refer to an activity that accountants once literally conducted for reasons that made sense at the time. The expression "keeping the books" is based on the now archaic practice of posting summaries of financial transactions in a series of books or ledgers, culminating in the "general ledger" that was used as a basis for preparing the financial statements.

➤ Yes, some of the old-time accountants did wear green eyeshades, probably because this gear made it easier to concentrate on the handwritten 14-column (or more) work papers then in common use. Accountants also operated adding machines with paper tapes, ideally entering the numbers without looking, and bulky calculators that took several seconds to grind out the answer when there was a need to multiply or divide.

➤ The advent of the computer led to the mechanization of large accounting systems on mainframe machines, and eventually desktop and laptop computers were developed for more specialized tasks. Today the large accounting systems have been linked together into all-inclusive corporate systems so that data need be entered only once.

Now close your eyes, and conjure up the Finance workplace of a bygone era. The first image is an accountant sitting on a high stool in a cramped little office (straight out of Dickens), adding and subtracting figures manually and writing entries in ledgers with a quill pen.

As organizations grew in size and complexity, Finance's activities expanded as well. Moreover, there were many innovations over the years.

Some forty years ago, the activities of Finance had become quite sophisticated, but remained labor-intensive. Reams of vouchers and other financial documents flowed in from the business units, where the cost accounting and other business level financial systems were maintained. Data from these systems had to be reviewed and then manually entered into corporate financial systems. Some of the corporate systems, such as fixed assets, were on the mainframe by then, which meant that data entry could be handled by key punch operators rather than accountants.

Much of the corporate-level work was done by groups of Finance people in large rooms located in the central office complex, sometimes referred to as "bullpens," under the watchful eye of several layers of supervision and management whose prime function was to ensure that accuracy was maintained. It took considerable time and effort to fill in worksheets by hand, add long columns of figures, calculate the percentages needed in financial reports, etc.

Analytical work was a luxury, performed primarily in response to requests from corporate management. With the exception of the internal auditors, who functioned as the corporate watchdogs, no one in Finance had much time or incentive to delve into whatever was happening in the businesses that might not be evident from the current financial numbers.

In most companies, the businesspeople believed that Finance was focused on the bottom line, and had little interest and limited competence in business matters. (How could people thought of in derogatory terms such as "bean counters" and "number crunchers" have any business competence?) Even when it came to investment proposals, Finance seemed less concerned with forecast assumptions than on whether the proposal was presented in the prescribed format and whether the numbers were internally consistent.

Businesspeople tended to view Finance as nothing but overhead and costs to be minimized (if not eliminated). They perceived that Finance people were only executors of tasks (collect the receivables, pay the payroll and suppliers, etc.), custodians of the company's assets, and historical financial reporters ("just keep the books and report the numbers"), with little else to contribute.

On top of these perceptions, Finance was engaged in adversarial processes with the businesses. Finance developed the targets for operating results and resources required, which meant that an allocation of resources and priorities among the various businesses was necessary. Not everyone was happy with the outcome. Finance demanded explanations for variances from plans for the last quarter and the comparable period of the prior year. Not everyone was happy to explain performance shortfalls. Finance drove programs (on behalf of corporate management) to reduce costs, people, and investments. Not everyone was happy with such programs and the consequent passing up of real opportunities.

Then there was the personal factor. Businesspeople saw no reason to seek the advice of Finance people, because they already understood financial matters from their own personal experiences, e.g., borrowing (taking out a mortgage), investing (calling a broker), and internal controls (reconciling a checkbook). How could what the Finance people do be any different or more complex?

The influence that Finance exercised in the scheme of things derived from association with corporate management. So long as there was support from management, Finance did not feel the need to justify its existence to the businesses. Thus, Finance would contact the businesses without necessarily indicating whether it was investigating a question from corporate management or whether it was simply seeking to prepare for a potential question. Either way, it was not apparent that Finance was adding much value to the situation.

The businesses suspected that any information they volunteered would be passed on with a Finance spin, which quite possibly would be negative, e.g., not in the budget, unwise increase in borrowings, numbers distorted by off-balance sheet financing, against company policy, or adverse tax consequences. Indeed, sometimes Finance passed on to senior corporate management (including the CEO) issues and plans before the business managers were ready to defend their ideas to their bosses. When a business manager said "we're getting a lot of help on this," the implication was typically just the opposite. In other words, the businesses did not trust Finance.

Small wonder that businesspeople were not particularly anxious to share information with Finance, let alone solicit its advice. If they did happen to need some financial information, it probably could not be obtained from Finance anyway. The perception was that Finance hoarded financial information as a source of power, and all too often this was true.

Last but not least, Finance people were perceived as backward looking and risk averse, and to some degree the reputation was deserved. Imagine the emphasis on the accuracy of monthly expense accruals, the annual fine-tuning of book depreciation rates, etc., all without any systematic effort to track what was happening to the economic value of the businesses.

Such complacency was possible in the era after World War II. Most U.S. companies relied principally on the domestic market, and did not face a great deal of international competition. Changes in the business world were not taking place nearly as fast as they have been in recent years, and shareholders tended to be far more patient.

The behaviors of the Finance people themselves had every bit as much to do with the negative perceptions of the old Finance as did the desires of businesspeople to purposely exclude them.

CFO: The old procedures and approaches are no longer viable, but Finance has changed with the times. Nowadays, I believe that we often have a clearer sense of the need for continuous improvement and growth than the businesspeople do.

CEO: That may be so, but negative stereotypes die hard, particularly when Finance people occasionally slip back into behaviors that reinforce them. Also, our society doesn't necessarily place a high value on some of the distinctive strengths of even the new Finance.

Consider the frequency of statements that Finance people are individually and collectively risk averse and focused on the preservation of capital rather than growth. Such perceptions are not necessarily fair. In many organizations, Finance has made great progress in assuming a value-adding role. However, surveys suggest that perceptions of Finance's role and mindset have changed much more within Finance itself than in the businesses.

The latter point is illustrated by Table 5-1, which is based on data from a poll conducted by Coopers & Lybrand:[1]

One reason for such a perception gap is that Finance people, by virtue of the role they play, sometimes have to take a stand. Finance is not always right, and even if Finance says "no" with good reason, there is bound to be disappointment and perhaps a perception that they just were not looking at things broadly enough.

Another point is that the predominant Finance mindset is methodical and logical, which means that one starts with the facts and figures and tries to work toward the best answer. Many people take a very different tack, making up their minds based on instinct and then looking for facts to support their conclusions. Generalizations are always dangerous, but this may help to explain why others whose minds work differently sometimes view Finance people as dull and unimaginative.

Just consider the traits and patterns that are held up as a model in contemporary society. While "IQ" was once revered, there is increasing emphasis on "emotional intelligence" and "people skills." "Right brain" thinking is in vogue; "left brain" thinking is out.

"Slow and steady" may win a lot of the races, as we all know, but the notion of instant success is more alluring. People fantasize about being discovered by a talent scout, making a bundle by day trading, winning the lottery, or welcoming the Publisher's Clearing House prize patrol.

Table 5-1. How Finance is perceived in an organization.

Question	Finance Manager Responses	General Manager Responses
Is the CFO a business partner?	Yes—28%	Yes—12%
Is the CFO involved with the business?	Yes—66%	Yes—25%
What is the CFO's primary role?	Business advocate —73%	Policeman—71%

The most influential sector of the media is not books or newspapers, but television, which prefers images and emotional content to information. A visitor from outer space might conclude that the heroes of our society are not the people who create the unprecedented wealth and prosperity that we enjoy, but rather athletes, singers, talk show hosts, movie stars, etc. Considering what some of these people earn, maybe it is true.

The working world is not entirely neglected on TV. Over the years there have been many shows about people at work, some of which seem realistic. Only a few occupations have been singled out for such attention, however, such as attorneys, police officers, doctors, and medical workers. Has there ever been a TV show about Finance people?

Perhaps this possibility has simply been overlooked, and "The Bottom Line" could be as big a hit as "The Practice," but probably not. A more likely inference is that the public relates to the stakes involved in certain types of legal work at an emotional level, but has no such reaction to the type of activities in which Finance people engage.

Indeed, business leaders in general do not come off very well in the media. Consider the popularity of the "Dilbert" comic strip, in which the pointy-headed boss constantly thwarts the efforts of everyone in the group that reports to him. There is just enough truth involved to make some of the episodes wickedly funny.

CFO: What can we do to change society's view?

CEO: All you can really do is work on perceptions of Finance within our company.

CFO: I can buy your picture of the old Finance, except that it doesn't seem to me Finance ever had much clout in the overall scheme of things.

CEO: Perhaps not, but Finance's influence was derived from corporate management and the businesspeople often thought that that kind of influence was considerable.

Perceptions are not necessarily reality, but people act in accordance with them all the same. If you do not expect that the person on the other end of the line will be receptive, it can be a real struggle to pick up the phone. Just imagine how stressful life must be for telemarketers. How often would any businessperson seek help from Finance if the answer was constantly that you cannot do something you want to do even if you believe it is right for your business?

Not only were Finance people seen as naysayers, but they always seemed to have a few aces up their sleeve in terms of being able to manipulate the numbers.

As the story goes, someone once asked several people what 1 + 1 equals. The teacher said 2, which is the answer in the book, and the mathematician agreed except that it could be plus 2 or minus 2 depending on the signs. The entrepreneur said 3, because there would surely be some synergy.

Then it was the accountant's turn, and yet another answer was suggested. "What number do you want?"

When a business proposal was rejected in the old days, it was not always easy to tell what had gone on behind the scenes. Corporate management might well have wielded the veto ax, but this was not necessarily apparent from the feedback provided, and it was only natural to harbor suspicions that Finance had played a hand in things.

Business managers who rose to the corporate management ranks certainly remembered where they had come from, and sometimes exerted their influence to raise the limits of delegated authority or curtail unpopular financial control procedures. This was just as well, because Finance could be mighty slow to propose needed changes on its own.

> Example: A while back, DuPont required the businesses to set "standards" for their inventories and accounts receivable in relation to business volume. The standards were reviewed and updated annually, and then sent to corporate management for approval in a consolidated report from Finance.
>
> The prime focus of the annual review was the inventory standards, which were calculated in terms of days' supply (DS) for all the major components of inventories.

DS often changed considerably from one year to the next. Finance spent approximately 4,000 staff hours per year on the working capital standards (WCS) report; countless additional hours were spent by the businesses.

Although the WCS review had a worthwhile purpose, namely ensuring that working capital levels were systematically monitored, the basic result was "acceptable" explanations for changes that were taking place anyway. The time focus (this year versus last year) and excessive level of detail tended to obscure rather than illuminate the effectiveness of inventory management. (For some of the businesses, a five-year trend line, for example, would have revealed an inventory buildup that was not clearly justified by the business circumstances.) No one could recall the disapproval of a proposed standard, and the Finance review mainly just refined the explanations.

One year, a new CEO held up a copy of the WCS report and asked whether anyone on the Executive Committee had any questions. No one spoke. Then he slid the report down the table to the secretary of the Committee with instructions to "file it." Finance submitted a greatly streamlined report the following year, and in due course working capital standards were eliminated altogether.

CFO: No doubt we have a few things to live down, but Finance has changed tremendously. In the old days, for instance, our answer to a misguided proposal might have been "no." Now we would say "that won't work because _____, but how can we help you achieve your objectives?"

CEO: That's an improvement, but don't forget that what people hear in a given situation is shaped by their perceptions. Maybe all the other person will remember from the exchange is "that won't work."

CFO: What if you got the word out that it's time to give Finance a chance?

CEO: That's what almost every group that comes to see me seems to wind up asking for, from quality and continuous improvement

to multicultural diversity. I think people overestimate my influence and underestimate the importance of winning voluntary acceptance.

CFO: How can we do that?

CEO: Finance is already working to upgrade the substance of what
it does, which is at least half the battle, but the approach needs to
be tailored to minimize resistance. If the businesspeople believe
that the new Finance agenda is to take over the company, which
is the impression that I was starting to get at our last meeting, the
shareholder value enabler thrust will be dead in the water.

CFO: That's certainly not our intent. What did I say that could have
suggested such an idea?

CEO: Just think of all the key tasks you were going to have Finance
handle. What would be left for the businesspeople to do, aside
from executing the strategies that Finance mapped out for them?

It is appropriate to quickly mention the suggestions the CFO earlier put on the table, with some conditions.

Upgrading the financial transaction groups is not a threat,
so long as the benefits are real and outweigh the potential gains
from continuing to drive cost reduction.

Integrating the budget process is a natural, because it not
only makes sense conceptually, but also addresses the very considerable degree of frustration that has built up with traditional
budgeting approaches.

Financial engineering is acceptable so long as deals are proposed to serve strategic business objectives. Technically ingenious solutions to problems that can be satisfactorily addressed
by conventional means are not likely to be welcome, and may
not prove beneficial.

The notion of having Finance take over competitive studies
and value chain analyses is problematic.

➤ Such studies have traditionally been the province of businesspeople in the organization, who typically are well suited by
experience and training to handle them from a conceptual standpoint. An offer by Finance to assume responsibility could easily
be perceived as a power grab.

➤ It is not apparent that bringing more quantitative rigor to such studies (the predictable result of turning them over to Finance) would necessarily be value-adding.

➤ There are other issues that Finance more urgently needs to address, many of which have been discussed.

If the business team wants a particular Finance person to handle or provide financial inputs on a competitive study or value chain analysis, that is an entirely different matter. Probably the Finance person and the person requesting the study will learn something from the project, the study output will be improved, and there will not be any negative perceptions about what is taking place.

CFO: I see where you're coming from, but it still seems to me that something is missing. Don't we need an affirmative sales pitch?

CEO: Yes, but it can't be a hard-sell approach. Imagine that Finance convened a meeting, explained that the company faced grave external challenges and needed to adapt or die, and then rattled off thirty-seven initiatives proposed for implementation in the next eighteen months. By the time the meeting was over, the presenters would be talking to an empty room.

If Finance really wants to implement their ideas about driving the creation of shareholder value throughout the company, they must first establish that there is a common problem and that everyone's input is needed to address it.

CFO: I'm finally starting to get the point. Do we also need to start changing some of the titles?

CEO: You bet! For starters, couldn't you do something about the "Controller" title?

It has been said that names are not important. After all, in the words of Shakespeare, a rose "by any other name would smell as sweet." Names, titles, and forms of address for human beings are loaded with significance, however, because of the emotional connotations.

Thus, the "Controller" title conveys the image of an authority figure whose influence may be exercised in a negative way.

Anyone who sees the flashing lights of a police car on the highway will instinctively let up on the accelerator—whether speeding or not—in their anxiety to avoid any contact with a "cop." Something similar occurs when the "Controller" approaches. It might be better to refer to the top corporate accountant as "Chief Accounting Officer" or "Director of Accounting."

The Finance label seems rather bland. Something catchier might be in order, such as Shareholder Value Enablers, but announcing that Finance should henceforth be referred to in this manner might seem presumptuous. It would probably be better to introduce this term as a reference to the intended future state.

Another issue is, Finance what? It is not a corporate department, division, or group, even if one exists, because there are also Finance people in the business units and outside the company. Moreover, there is no good reason to emphasize the organizational boundaries that continue to exist within the company because they may not be there forever.

Calling Finance a function is not right either, because it is actually a diverse collection of business activities. There is no real need for a second word to be added to the Finance name. It should be sufficient to simply refer to "Finance" or "Shareholder Value Enablers" (SVE for short), with the latter name gradually supplanting the former to help foster a perception change.

Last but not least, the distinction between "operating" and "staff" functions should be dropped from the corporate vocabulary. "Staff" has come to have a derogatory and subservient implication. Even if this were not so, it would be counterproductive to make such a distinction between groups of employees that should be working together.

For essentially the same reasons, it would be best to stop talking about internal customers versus internal suppliers and profit centers versus cost centers. Shareholder value creators/shareholder value enablers at least captures the idea of a partnership of diverse talents to serve a common objective without highlighting the distinction between one side of the partnership and the other.

CFO: Anything else?

CEO: Yes, you need a substitute for "a seat at the decision-making table." Choose something that doesn't sound so self-interested.

CFO: I'd like to mull that one over. How would it be if we adjourn until next week?

CEO: Fine, see you then.

Summing Up

➤ Businesspeople have been traditionally reluctant to have Finance participate in their affairs, for which reason they created a Finance-avoidance culture. Their perceptions that Finance has been backward looking, unduly risk averse, and out of touch with the businesses were often justified.

➤ A Finance-avoidance culture developed because Finance was focused on specialized tasks and routines that were primarily directed to the financial control of the businesses, and because the behavior of Finance people toward businesspeople promoted such a culture.

➤ The influence of Finance was derived from corporate management, and tended to be resented rather than appreciated by the businesspeople. Finance did not see a need to justify its existence to the businesses, which fed into the resentment.

➤ The work procedures and mindset of Finance have changed in recent years, but old perceptions die hard. To make the jump to a shareholder value enabler role, Finance must first change its behavior in order to establish a new and more positive image.

➤ Calling Finance by a new name—Shareholder Value Enablers or "SVE"—facilitates changing perceptions.

Notes

1. Thomas Walther et al. (Coopers & Lybrand), *Reinventing the CFO: Moving from Financial Management to Strategic Management* (New York: McGraw-Hill, 1997), 19.

Chapter Six

THE NEW BUSINESS-FINANCE PARTNERSHIP

First and foremost, treat others as you expect to be treated and respect everyone as an equal.

Lisa Daniel McAdams, WorldCom, Inc., 1990s[1]

CEO: When we last talked you were going to revisit the Finance vision, and perhaps reformulate it. What did you come up with?

CFO: I believe that what we need is a partnership with the businesses to drive shareholder value throughout the company. If such a partnership can be put in place, a seat for Finance at the decision-making table will take care of itself. In other words, we would be Shareholder Value Enablers or simply SVE.

Let other organizations maintain their Finance-avoidance and Finance-function cultures if they want to, but such subcultures are a costly anachronism that an enlightened company can no longer afford. Now is the time for the businesses and Finance to join forces, so that together they can seize competitive advantage in a fast moving business and financial world.

The businesses have much to offer and so does Finance. The partnership will be stronger if they maintain their separate identities and roles, but they still need to dismantle the barriers that have prevented a full-fledged partnership in the past.

Both sides will need to compromise, so that together they can achieve their goals—through *Partnering for Performance* (PFP).

CEO: If someone could bottle that type of thinking, I'd like to put it in the drinking water. But there must be a catch. Are we going to have to reorganize again?

CFO: Not necessarily. Let's get straight that we're not talking about reengineering processes or even reinventing the company. These are not partnering initiatives, but efficiency thrusts. The real need is to change the culture, so that partnering will flourish, which will require adjustments by both the businesses and SVE.

Organizational structure reflects the intended alignment of resources with strategy. It follows that no particular organizational structure can be identified as a best practice model, any more than there is one ideal corporate strategy.

Successful companies can be highly centralized, highly decentralized, or fall somewhere in between. Some are organized by product line, some by customers or market segments, and some by geographical areas. If the CEO is trying to drive more than one orientation simultaneously, a company may be matrix-managed with key employees reporting to two bosses (e.g., product line manager on a solid line and country manager on a dotted line, or vice versa).

Many companies have tried different organizational structures over time. The CEO will often reorganize a company shortly after taking the helm, or when the company is trying something new, to facilitate the desired changes.

Example: At one time, the business activities of DuPont in Europe, Latin America, and the Far East were managed by the International Department, which reported the associated sales, earnings, and investment as one of the company's profit centers. Initially, the primary focus of the international business was the resale of products manufactured in the United States on a basically opportunistic basis, although there were also some offshore manufacturing operations.

As the international business became an increasingly important part of the company's total business, there were demands from the International Department for dedicated production capacity, technical support, and personnel for international assignments. The domestic businesses were reluctant to help because they were not getting credit for international sales and earnings.

To continue DuPont's transition into a truly global company, corporate management redefined the role of the International Department (initially for Europe, later for other areas) from having profit and loss responsibility to providing liaison and country infrastructure. Meanwhile, the domestic businesses were given worldwide (domestic and offshore) responsibility for managing their product lines.

Regardless of an organization's size or structure, it should be possible to establish partnering relationships. The key is to work on the internal culture—defined here as the way people in the organization work together to achieve shared goals, objectives, and aspirations.

Every organization has a distinctive culture, which reflects the beliefs and values that are explicitly or implicitly recognized within its confines. Some organizational cultures are better than others, and one can discern points to emulate or avoid by observing them. Thus:

➤ It seems right to be respectful of individual feelings and aspirations rather than rigidly imposing the views of the majority.

➤ A heavy emphasis on restricting the internal flow of information to those with a "need to know" can prove nonproductive.

Still, organizations have succeeded with a variety of cultures, which reflect their history, present circumstances, and objectives. No organization's culture is optimal. Indeed, designating any state of being as ideal (versus pretty good for now) ignores the need to continue to improve things.

Some believe that company values are so important that they drive the results of business operations. In accordance with this thinking, a number of companies have developed formal statements of their values that everyone is expected to honor and observe.

Example: In 1984, Roy Haas became CEO of Levi Strauss, a long-time manufacturer of blue jeans that had experienced reverses starting in the late 1970s. The company was taken private in a 1985 leveraged buy-out, and faced the dual challenge of improving its operating results and servicing the heavy debt load that had been assumed.

Haas led the company through a wrenching downsizing, and also supported the development of an Aspirations Statement to summarize the company's ideals and values. His thinking was that the employees closest to the product and the customers should be empowered to make more decisions in a stretched and flattened organization, so long as such decisions were in accordance with the company's strategies and values.

Among other things, the Aspirations Statement called for "new behaviors," which were described as follows:

Leadership that exemplifies directness, openness to influence, commitment to the success of others, willingness to acknowledge our own contributions to problems, personal accountability, teamwork, and trust. Not only must we model these behaviors but we must coach others to adopt them.[2]

Whether or not a company's values should be formally written down and published, which demonstrates their perceived importance but may have the unintended effect of enshrining them and discouraging future improvement, any company seriously interested in driving PFP should begin by looking inward at the currently existing culture (or subcultures).

CEO: You said earlier that both the businesses and Finance will need to change. What's involved for the businesses?
CFO: Basically, the Finance-avoidance culture must be replaced by a new and more constructive view of SVE.

When you get right down to it, the Finance-avoidance culture has been perpetuated by negative perceptions. To a large extent, these perceptions are not based on the present-day behaviors and mindset of Finance, but on things that happened years ago. In other words, they are based on emotion rather than fact and logic.

As for the need to change, it can hardly be denied that everyone in a company is in the same boat. Investors are looking for an attractive return on their investments, and expect to get it. If the company's performance suffers because the business and Finance people cannot get along, the shareholders will not care which side is more deserving of blame.

If the negative perceptions about Finance are justified, it is up to SVE to do something about them. Otherwise, both the businesses and SVE should check these ideas at the door.

The "operating" (or "line") versus "staff" distinction may have some value in a military context, but is out of place in an economic enterprise. Whether the "staff" people are viewed as extra special because their power and prestige emanate from corporate management, or second-class citizens because they are not out calling on customers every day, it is contrary to the idea of partnering to stress that different classes of people are involved.

The notion of "internal customers" served by "internal suppliers" implies a superior and subordinate relationship even more surely than the "line" versus "staff" distinction, and should be rejected for the same reason. The suggested distinction is also illogical, because it is not the so-called "customers" who pay for the services rendered. Only real customers pay cash.

It is common to view Finance groups as "cost centers," while the businesses are perceived as "profit centers." What one wants to do with costs, all else being equal, is to reduce or eliminate them. In other words, the emphasis on continuous cost reduction remains prevalent even though there may be far greater potential gains from enhancing the value-adding side of the equation.

Actually, the businesses are no more "profit centers" than Finance is, because every activity within the company represents cost rather than profit. As Peter Drucker put it:

> *There are no profit centers within the business; there are only cost centers. The only thing one can say with certainty about any business activity, whether engineering or selling, manufacturing or accounting, is that it consumes efforts and thereby incurs costs. Whether it contributes to results remains to be seen.*
>
> *Results depend not on anybody within the business nor on anything within the control of the business. They depend on somebody outside—the customer in a market economy, the political authorities in a controlled economy. It is always somebody outside who decides whether the efforts of a business become economic results or whether they become so much waste and scrap.*[3]

Nothing is to be gained from classifying business activities as low value-added versus high value-added, strategic versus tactical, or essential versus nonessential. It is quite true that some activities have more leverage to influence a company's overall results than others do. Some of the highest-leverage activities are financial in nature, but there is no need to emphasize it.

A tax analyst may be able to save more money with one idea than a top sales representative could earn for the company in years (after-tax profit margin is generally only 5 to 10 percent of sales), but both are doing a job that needs to be done. If someone is adding value, they deserve to be treated with respect and encouraged to do even better, not told that they are unimportant to the company. As for the nonessential people, how come they are still around?

The new partnering culture is much easier to describe, because there are not as many labels. It is all about being in the same boat, rowing together to move it in the right direction, and being equally responsible for arriving at the intended destination.

CEO: OK, how does Finance need to change?
CFO: SVE must break out of its functional excellence box, and get more comfortable working with undefined space. Charles Handy illustrated this point with a donut concept.

Driving for functional excellence has taken Finance a long way. It is something that Finance people understand very well, and are good at doing. The natural tendency is to keep doing it, with further gains clearly in view, but this is the path to suboptimization.

Finance people are well aware that their activities must complement and reinforce the activities of the businesspeople, the leaders of the businesses and company, and the CEO. Consider how readily Finance people bought into the internal supplier and internal customer model, which in effect relieves Finance of responsibility. "Don't ask me why the business team wants that report, that's what they asked for."

It is becoming increasingly evident, however, that Finance activities can add more value if they are conducted in a partnering rather than subordinate capacity. "This report would make much more sense if it came out annually instead of monthly and was tied to the NPV projection. Don't you agree?"

Inevitably, a partnering relationship entails acceptance of the challenges of growth and uncertainty. These conditions, which will affect all organizational relationships in the future, have been well described by Charles Handy (see Figure 6-1).[4]

Handy conceptualizes work as an inside-out donut, with the solid core being basic responsibilities and the hole around it undefined workspace.

Figure 6-1. Charles Handy's work-donut concept.

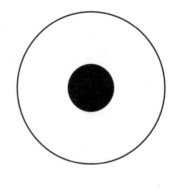

He suggests that the balancing of the core (what must be done) with that which lies beyond (what could be done) is the key to organizational and personal success.

In a knowledge-based and partnering organization, the solid part of the donut will shrink over time as employees become more cost and time efficient in carrying out well-defined tasks and responsibilities. Meanwhile, the hole expands as employees learn to add value and promote growth in a business and financial world that is changing with unprecedented speed. For partnering to flourish in an organization, it is imperative that everyone be comfortable with undefined space in which roles and responsibilities are not rigidly defined, and that all partners be equally responsible for working to achieve outcomes.

To partner with the businesses and assume a true Shareholder Value Enablers role, Finance must move beyond the comfort zone of well-defined financial activities (its core) into the new, fast-changing world (undefined space) that lies beyond. This in turn will require a new mindset that SVE is willing to embrace *and* practice.

Partnering is really a reflection of an organization's values (e.g., trust, information sharing, reliance on one another). Here are some of the new beliefs and values about SVE that must replace the Finance-avoidance and Finance-function subcultures of the past, including real life examples:

1. *SVE people are first and foremost businesspeople, and are financial specialists second.* They offer expertise about financial matters, based on their education and experience, just as other businesspeople can offer expertise in sales, marketing, manufacturing, or technology. Everyone in the enterprise is a businessperson, however, and SVE people are keenly aware of how their efforts fit into the overall scheme of things.

> Example: Diane Dutton became CFO of Allstate Rental and Car Sales in 1998 after a series of accounting assignments with a variety of businesses. She attributes her success to an ability to not only understand the numbers but see beyond them. "I'm a sponge. I listen, ask questions, go into warehouses, talk to people working on the line, and go after customers. When I was working for a medical equipment company, for example, I learned all I could about IV pumps, heart machines, and the length of hospital stays. I try to sponge up everything I can about an industry."[5]

SVE plays an invaluable role in accumulating financial and operating numbers for the businesses, organizing the raw numbers (data) into an understandable form (information), and assessing the information to derive insightful conclusions (knowledge) that can be shared with business partners and profitably applied.

Numbers come in many forms and serve a variety of purposes. There are financial numbers (e.g., performance versus budget) and operating numbers (e.g., yield per unit); both can cover the short or long term. Numbers can be reported as such, in text, columns, or tables, or used as the basis for graphs and charts. Some numbers are absolute values, while others are fractions or ratios (e.g., profit margin).

Regardless of their type or form, all numbers require interpretation to be useful to the businesses and SVE must help with the interpretations. Without a common language, organizational knowledge is impossible.

2. *SVE people are equal contributors.* The functions of an organization are like cinderblocks in a dam. If a block in any part of the dam weakens under pressure and fails, the valley is flooded. Similarly, no organization can fully achieve its objectives if any one of its functions is weak. Any activity that is superfluous must be jettisoned for the sake of productivity and efficiency, and all of the activities that remain—which most assuredly includes SVE—are to be highly prized.

> Example: ITT Industries, Inc., one of the companies created by the 1995 split-up of ITT (see Chapter 3), was still a highly diversified enterprise. Its business portfolio included semiconductors, automotive parts, Florida real estate, and much more. Heidi Kunz was brought in as CFO from General Motors, and championed a shareholder value perspective throughout the company. She also assumed responsibility for the divestiture of most of the company's automotive units, two of which were sold to European purchasers in 1998 for a total of $3.6 billion. Kunz became an executive vice president, with line responsibility for the automotive businesses that were retained

3. *SVE people are customer-focused.* Although Finance people do not typically call on the company's customers, they look for ways to become auxiliary members of the sales and marketing team.

One of the prerequisites for any organization's survival is obtaining revenues to cover the costs of its internal operations and financing. Every employee, regardless of assignment, needs to be customer-focused. That is, every employee—and SVE people are no exception—must always consider how best to help increase revenues. After all, any business will fail if its revenues are insufficient, no matter how worthwhile its objectives.

Many opportunities to develop a customer focus are available to SVE people; all it takes is a little creativity.

Example: The CFO of Nortel Networks initiated personal relationships with the CFOs of the company's largest customers in North America, Europe, and Asia. These customers represented more than half of the company's worldwide business. The purpose of this initiative was to establish another means of access to the customer than the usual marketing and purchasing relationship, which could be used to generate business or resolve issues.

Although this alternative door was not used often, the businesses (and presumably the customers) appreciated knowing that it existed. There were also frequent communications with the customer CFOs regarding financial matters of common interest, such as FASB pronouncements and IRS rulings.

As an extension of this initiative, the CFO arranged a conference for the CFOs of Nortel's ten largest U.S. customers—the seven (at the time) Baby Bells, GTE, MCI, and Sprint—by putting together an agenda that attracted them. (Eight of the ten CFOs were able to attend.) Denny Beresford, chairman of the FASB, as well as the CEO of a large Wall Street investment bank, a leading economist, a prominent securities analyst, and others, were on the program. Although there were no free afternoons, the three-day session was a big hit, and the CFOs "voted" to do it again in the future.

There is also no shortage of market focus opportunities in lower levels of organizations for those who look for them.

Example: One of the credit representatives at Nortel took it upon herself to solve a major collection problem by visiting a consistently late-paying customer. It turned out that the problem was poor billing accuracy. Working first with the customer to determine its needs and then with Nortel's billing group, she was able to resolve the billing problem (and, thus, the collection problem) quickly as well as ensure a happy customer.

Similarly, many opportunities exist for CFOs and members of their teams to build relationships with their counterparts at suppliers, joint venture partners, etc., again with mutually beneficial results.

4. *SVE people bring unique perspectives to the decision-making table.* A healthy diversity of backgrounds, expertise, contacts, and ideas strengthens an organization and improves its decision-making process. (Said another way, two heads are better than one in solving problems.) The importance of this principle can only grow in an increasingly complex, fast-moving, and global business environment.

> Example: In any competitive setting, there is strength in diversity. For instance, the Denver Broncos were the Super Bowl champions in 1998 and 1999. Much credit was given to quarterback John Elway, and deservedly so, but the team would not have done very well with fifty-three all-star quarterbacks. To win the championship, it needed talent at every position, namely running backs, fullbacks, wide receivers, tight ends, interior linemen, defensive linemen, linebackers, cornerbacks, safeties, punters, place-kickers, and special teams.

Also note that some people can contribute more than thought possible, if given a chance to perform in a different role.

The value of diversity has long been recognized, even in the days when the "captains of industry" were calling most of the shots. Diversity was thought of then in terms of functional expertise, youth versus experience, and differing ideas. Effective managers might encourage the expression of contrary views just to test the group's thinking.

> Example: Alfred Sloan, who took over a collection of acquired automobile companies that was on the verge of collapse in 1921 and molded General Motors into a highly successful business enterprise, is reported to have said at a meeting of one of his top committees: "Gentlemen, I take it we are all in complete agreement on the decision here."

Everyone around the table nodded assent. "Then," continued Sloan, "I propose we postpone further discussion of this matter until our next meeting to give ourselves time to develop disagreement and perhaps gain some understanding of what the decision is all about."[6]

In recent years, the principle of diversity has been extended to such areas as gender, race, socioeconomic class, and nationality. Such an extension is the right thing to do, and good business besides. Perhaps a global business could be run with people from only one country, but this is hardly the best way to go about things. Similarly, a team of people may have great difficulty understanding a market if its members are representative of only one or two of the market's segments.

Communications is the glue that binds the members of a partnership together. (A failure to communicate effectively can lead to war, divorce, and litigation.) When PFP is an organizational reality, SVE can share not only financial expertise but also several perspectives that are not generally available to businesspeople. These include:

➤ *Internal perspectives to the businesses.* In the course of fulfilling its duties (from collecting data to generating reports), SVE works with all units in an organization. It therefore becomes familiar with accomplishments, failures, strategies, plans, financial results and projections—or in other words what does and does not work.

➤ *Corporate perspectives to the businesses.* To determine the overall organizational numbers or outcomes, SVE must consolidate and assess the results, plans, projections, etc., of the individual businesses. The resulting knowledge is available for sharing with the business units. In addition, because SVE people are in regular communication with the board of directors, the CEO, and other senior managers, they can often keep the individual businesses posted on the perspectives, concerns, reasons for actions, and plans of the organizational leadership.

➤ *External perspectives to the businesses.* SVE communicates regularly with more outside parties than anyone else, with the possible exception of the CEO. (Appendix C lists the wide range of people with whom the typical CFO communicates.) Among such parties are bankers, securities analysts, independent accountants, and other outside groups in a position to objectively view the organization vis-à-vis its competitors. Besides being potential sources of competitive business intelligence, such contacts can provide suggestions for improving performance, insights on how other organizations are addressing a given issue, and input on trends in the business and financial world.

5. *SVE people have a proper sense of urgency.* The longer it takes to do something, the more cost will accumulate and the more opportunities there will be for mistakes (e.g., excessive analysis of multiple-choice questions is unlikely to improve one's score). Moreover, there is an opportunity cost for failing to strike while the iron is hot. By the time a long-delayed decision is implemented, it may be obsolete and therefore useless. In today's competitive environment, no organization can afford to incur unnecessary costs, especially if they are self-inflicted.

Business partners must not waste time or squander opportunities by endless debates, and no one is in a better position to remind everyone of this imperative than the SVE partner.

Example: Many years ago, a young Finance manager of DuPont was transferred into an area in which a proposed financial initiative had been under study for several years. The reasons for implementation had been well documented and appeared overwhelming, so he drafted a report seeking approval to proceed. His superior agreed with the thrust of the report, but was concerned by the question, "If this is such a good idea, why didn't we do it earlier?" It was suggested that submission and approval of the report should be coordinated with the travel and vacation schedules of various executives who might be interested.

Checking the calendar for the next several months, no submission date could be identified that was in synch with everyone's schedule. The Finance manager observed that he had read how the planets line up approximately once a century, and that the matter at hand appeared to be of a similar nature. The report went in the following week and was approved without incident.

6. *SVE people are innovative.* In a rapidly changing business environment, traditional conclusions about familiar subjects may well have become outmoded. Whether dealing with business or financial issues, SVE people are willing to "think outside the box" when the occasion requires to arrive at better answers.

Doing the same thing all the time can become boring after a while, and also ensures mediocrity. "If you always do what you always did," as the saying goes, "you'll always get what you always got," and that is just not good enough! In contrast, thinking in new ways and learning new skills can be very pleasurable and challenging.

Internal controls were traditionally thought of as a means to safeguard company assets, for instance, and as such are not highly valued by businesspeople. Today, internal controls can be viewed as measures that help businesspeople run their businesses, i.e., provide more accurate information that will improve decision making. In this light, they should be more warmly accepted rather than being viewed as restraints, and they should work better because everyone is actively supporting them.

One way to identify areas where new thinking is needed is to hold a needs assessment discussion with some of the businesspeople. An SVE partner could ask the business partners for a list of the ten financial practices that they think could be better handled or eliminated, and their ten needs for financial support not currently being met. Then after investigation and reflection, the SVE partner would suggest changes to be implemented and explain why other changes were not possible. Imagine the understanding among the partners that would be generated.

7. *SVE is committed to high ethical standards.* Ultimately, it is individuals who make the decisions that determine any organization's success and reputation. Together with other members of the business team, SVE must strive to ensure that the com-

pany's activities are conducted in a manner that is above reproach.

Allegations that a company has engaged in price-fixing, marketed an unsafe product, misstated earnings, cheated on its taxes, overcharged on government contracts, concealed environmental problems, etc., can be devastating, especially if they prove to be well founded. Analogous exposures exist in government and non-profit organizations. For instance, disclosures of campaign finance violations or personal misconduct can be ruinous in the governmental sector.

It would be impracticable to commit that the company will never act in a manner that could conceivably be challenged in the light of some law, regulation, or social expectation. Also, there is likely to be at least one "bad apple" in a large group of people. SVE can and does commit, however, that:

➤ No action will be taken or condoned in the name of the company that cannot be squared with a reasonable interpretation of the existing requirements, and with a willingness to have full public disclosure.

➤ The company will refrain from actions that seem ethically dubious or unfair, even if there is "no law against it."

When in doubt, a good question to ask oneself might be: "Would I (and my family and friends) be proud to read about what I've decided in the local newspaper or see it on the 11:00 news?" If the answer is no, reconsider. Not only is such a question useful in clarifying one's thinking, but, depending on how things go, it may not be purely hypothetical.

If a decision does wind up being disclosed and critiqued in the public arena, any potential adverse impact on the company will be minimized by facing up to the issue forthrightly. Indeed, clear actions and plain talk are generally the most effective approach to any high-profile issue, no matter who is to blame.

Example: Johnson & Johnson was faced with a nightmarish problem when, on two occasions, unrelated persons laced stocks of Tylenol with cyanide, resulting in the deaths of a total of eight people. On both occasions, the company moved swiftly to publicize the problem and recall Tylenol supplies from store shelves around the country. Such action exemplified Johnson & Johnson's "customer first" credo, and contributed to the outstanding reputation that the company enjoys today.

There are many cases of improper decisions that have landed people and organizations in hot water. There are also many cases where a person acted with courage and conviction to avoid such problems. Often such a person must remain an unsung hero to avoid embarrassment to others, but here is one story that is old enough to be told:

Example: One day, DuPont's corporate controller read in the Wall Street Journal of an accounting irregularity at another company, and asked the tax group to determine whether DuPont had any similar problems.

It turned out that a few of the businesses had been systematically expensing a portion of plant investment before consumption took place. Although the resulting understatement of income was only a timing difference, it was clearly contrary to both financial and tax reporting requirements. The amounts involved were promptly determined, capitalized in the year's financial statements with appropriate disclosure, and reported to the IRS—a fine example of the controller's philosophy that Finance should serve as the "conscience of the company."

8. *SVE people work hard at what they do, but they also have fun.* Think of all the hours that someone spends on the job during a career. Not to have fun would be a personal tragedy.

This is not meant to suggest that your job should not be taken seriously, far from it, but it is OK to lighten up. There is no need to wear a three-piece suit on "casual Fridays," or take home a briefcase full of weekend reading when what you really need is a break to recharge your creative batteries. Moreover, having fun will enhance one's ability to achieve goals and objectives, both personally and in a partnering relationship.

Enthusiasm is contagious. A team of people with diverse talents working together to solve a problem may find great satisfaction in a job well done, and it is always a good idea to savor the moment before moving on to new challenges.

> Example: When DuPont sent a new Finance manager to its Brazilian subsidiary some time ago, he found that its operations were in the red. One of the contributing factors was that financing expense (which was quite substantial given the applicable inflation rate) was being treated as a corporate charge. As a result, some of the businesses that were considered profitable were actually operating in the red.
>
> The newcomer vigorously championed the need for profits on a net basis, and the businesses began to pare the losses. One magic day, the monthly results were announced at a social function—for the first time there was a real profit and a nice one at that. "Finance cooked the books," quipped one the business managers, but everyone knew the result was real and they had achieved it. There was a lot of pride (and fun) in that room.

CEO: I support your suggestions, but the idea of more and more undefined space worries me. How do we know that all of it will be filled productively?

CFO: Don't forget that the unfilled portion of the Handy donut represents activities and behaviors that are new and unfamiliar, not slack time. Given the challenge of continually increasing shareholder value while keeping all the other stakeholders happy, I don't think anyone will have too much time to get into trouble.

As has often been noted, there is a law of diminishing returns in both business and the world in general. So it is far easier to pick the low hanging fruit than to go for the last apple or two on the top of the tree.

People in organizations will remain busy doing something, whether or not their efforts are productive. Peter Drucker once suggested that this problem may be particularly marked in the case of highly trained people because of their pride in doing the difficult—whether productive or not.

In a knowledge-based economy, however, the real source of a company's competitive advantage may be the creative thinking that someone is doing while they appear to be gazing out the window or are not present in the workplace at all. Do not dismiss a statement that "the idea came to me while I was taking a walk before breakfast," because this might be exactly what happened. Legend has it that Isaac Newton conceived of the theory of gravitation after an apple fell on his head.

The challenge would seem to be striking a proper balance. There must be enough tension in the workplace to keep employees goal-directed, which ideally should be self-induced, but not so much as to eliminate their thinking time and drive out creativity.

Despite the tendency of familiar core activities to occupy a shrinking share of total work activity, it is not uncommon for employees in companies with challenging performance goals and a partnering culture to find themselves working harder than ever.

Example: At Nucor Corporation, a steel "minimill" that has achieved rapid growth by becoming the low cost steel producer in the United States, one of the divisional controllers reported spending "between 10 to 15 percent of my time on accounting functions [backed up by a full-time accountant]" and said that "most of my time is spent in the purchasing function, negotiations, legal issues, and personnel issues."[7]

If anything, the problem is not that people will not keep busy, but that new tasks of a tactical nature will tend to crowd out more strategic endeavors as SVE people are asked to take on new financial responsibilities. Ideally, the SVE people of the future should spend an increasing share of their time in:

> building new constituencies (e.g., reaching out to others, both within and outside the organization, and offering help)

> engaging in new and broadening activities (e.g., learning how to solve business versus purely financial problems)

> assuming new and contribution-enlarging responsibilities (e.g., educating business partners about financial tools and techniques)

For readers of this book who have subordinates in the workplace, here is an exercise that could prove enlightening and useful. (A similar approach was suggested earlier in this chapter in reference to partnering.) The premises are that no one knows a job better than the person who is doing it, and that everyone likes to be consulted.

Call in each of your subordinates, and ask them to develop two lists:

> Ten things about their jobs that are either dissatisfying or nonproductive, and which they don't believe need to be done.

> Ten things they could do that would add value, but have been told not to do or do not have time to handle.

Thoughtfully review the lists that are submitted, talk to whomever you need to, and then provide specific feedback. You might respond that four items on the first list can be discontinued immediately, one is to comply with SEC reporting requirements, three are needed because the business team uses the information to do XYZ, and two are questionable and need to be discussed further. There would be a similar response to the second list, e.g., "let's do five of the items starting now, two are possible but require further study, one needs to be clarified, and two will not fly because of ABC."

This approach is hardly rocket science, but you may be surprised at what it can do for the morale, efficiency, and effectiveness of the people that you are depending on to get the job done. Imagine what would be learned and what the cumulative impact could be if all the managers in an organization were doing the same thing, and as a result, without any drastic change, all of the employees were motivated to improve their performance just a little bit every day.

CEO: What kind of guarantee will you offer that the new Finance or SVE can deliver?

CFO: Initially, the businesses will have to take this on faith, but a Partnering for Performance or PFP relationship between the businesses and SVE is a low-risk bet that could pay off handsomely. There's no incremental cost as Finance people are already on the payroll, and they could turn out to be a stalwart ally in the unending battle for competitive advantage.

It is not the premise of this book that SVE alone can create shareholder value, but it can be a powerful catalyst and influence in the shareholder value-creation process. SVE must therefore break out of the Porter box of financial efficiency, so as to become an important source of competitive business advantage.

Skeptics may agree in theory, but suggest that SVE will not make a real competitive difference in the long run. After all, a value-adding role for SVE can and probably will be emulated by competitors. Perhaps so, but the same thing could be said about any source of competitive advantage. Besides, other organizations may not catch on right away, given the well-known resistance to change. As Niccolo Machiavelli noted some 500 years ago, "there is nothing more difficult to take in hand, more perilous to conduct, or more uncertain in its success, than to take the lead in the introduction of a new order of things."[8]

The new SVE role is more than anything else a new way of thinking and behaving, not unlike any other business competency that is core to the organization. Some organizations capitalize on the competitive advantage from such competencies quicker, and sustain them more effectively, than others, and they are the ones that will survive and prosper in the new millennium.

CEO: Looks like we're out of time again, but let me ask one more question. Assuming that Partnering for Performance is a great idea, and I believe it is, how are we going to implement it?

CFO: The first step is to develop some meaningful success stories, which will give everyone an idea of what they can accomplish in the new culture. Then we must make sure that the company's goals and incentives are in synch, and nature will take its course. I'll get into some specifics next week.

SUMMING UP

➤ Partnering for Performance (PFP) is a new way for the businesses and Finance to team up and drive the creation of shareholder value. It can be implemented in all types of organizations, regardless of their size or structure.

➤ The businesses must give up their Finance-avoidance culture, and buy into new beliefs, e.g., that Finance people are first and foremost businesspeople who can contribute equal value.

➤ Finance must give up its old mindset of driving functional excellence, and become comfortable with undefined space. This will require working with new constituencies on new activities with a new sense of responsibilities.

➤ PFP creates opportunities for SVE to more effectively dialogue with the businesses by providing fresh perspectives (internal, external, and corporate) on the organization and the changing world outside.

➤ PFP is a low-risk bet, with a large potential payoff, for companies that embrace it quickly and implement it effectively.

NOTES

1. A. Mikaelian, *Women Who Mean Business: Success Stories of Women Over 40* (New York: William Morrow and Company, 1999), 172.

2. Henry A. Davis and Frederick C. Militello, *The Empowered Organization: Redefining the Roles and Practices of Finance* (Morristown, New Jersey: Financial Executives Research Foundation, 1994), 151–169. Reprinted with permission from Financial Executives Research Foundation, Inc.

3. Peter F. Drucker, *The Executive in Action* (from *Managing for Results, 1964*), (New York: HarperBusiness/ HarperCollins Publishers, 1996), 17. Copyright © 1966, 1967 by Peter F. Drucker. Copyright renewed 1994, 1995 by Peter F. Drucker. Reprinted by permission of HarperCollins Publishers, Inc.

4. Charles Handy, *The Age of Paradox* (Boston: Harvard Business School Press, 1995), 69–86.

5. Mikaelian, op. cit., 231.

6. Drucker, op. cit., 672.

7. Stephen F. Jablonsky and Patrick J. Keating, *Changing Roles of Financial Management: Integrating Strategy, Control, and Accountability* (Morristown, New Jersey: Financial Executives Research Foundation, 1998), 82–83. Reprinted with permission from Financial Executives Research Foundation, Inc.

8. John Bartlett, *Familiar Quotations* (Boston: Little, Brown and Company, 1980), 153:18.

Chapter Seven

IMPLEMENTING
PARTNERING FOR
PERFORMANCE

A journey of a thousand miles must begin with a single
step—but it must be in the right direction.

Lao-tzu, circa 550 B.C., with a modern twist

CEO: Let me ask you a question before you get into the PFP implementation plan. Aside from making sure that the company isn't
going off in several directions at once, why is it so important to
get the business and SVE people working together?

CFO: Together they will be more capable of venturing into unex-
plored territory and more likely to understand what they find
there in time to do something about it.

When it was published in 1990, *The Fifth Discipline: The Art and
Science of the Learning Organization* met with a warm recep-
tion. The reason was that author Peter Senge had pointed out a
new path to the corporate Holy Grail of sustainable competitive
advantage.

In a dynamic and competitive world, no organization—

however successful it may be—can afford to slavishly follow its tried and true course. Inevitably, someone else will learn a better way, and put it into practice. Only a learning organization can keep improving on its successes and keep learning from and correcting its mistakes: That's how it survives.

This is not to say that organizations are truly "cognitive beings." To the contrary, all of the learning takes place in the minds of individual human beings. Even the knowledge that winds up being recorded in a company's computer programs, technical manuals, business files, etc., has no meaning except when accessed by people. (Things may change considerably when computers learn to think, but that probably will not happen for another fifty years or so.)

How does one go about creating a learning organization? There are all sorts of theories—wheels of learning, shared mental models, ladders of inference, archetypes, microworlds, safe havens, parallel systems, and so on.[1] It would be surprising if the employees of an organization could develop a common understanding of how to implement such concepts. Even if they did, they might well forget in the process that knowledge has no real value unless it is acted on.

Perhaps a simpler model will suffice for purposes of implementing PFP. It is based on the Johari Window that psychologists Joe Luft and Harry Ingham developed in the 1950s to represent the common, separate and unperceived areas in human relationships,[2] but has been modified to depict a functional interface.

Imagine a window with four panes (see Figure 7–1). The business team (other than Finance) can see through the bottom two panes, whereas the view through the left two panes is visible only to Finance. There is an area of overlap representing common knowledge, and an area that neither of the partners can clearly perceive.

Note that the greatest opportunities are likely to reside in the unknown, if for no other reason than because that is where companies without PFP will find it the most difficult to go. As for the reasons to go there, Thomas Jefferson put it this way in 1817: "Knowledge is power, knowledge is safety, knowledge is happiness."

Figure 7-1. Variation of a Johari Window.

Finance View	The Unknown
Common Knowledge	Business View

CEO: Let's play with that idea. I realize that SVE people are adept with numbers and may have some good input about internal and external developments picked up through their contacts with other groups, but they hardly have a monopoly on such knowledge.

CFO: Granted, but SVE people tend to pick up and process information in a different way. The best way that I can describe it is that businesspeople are passionate about their businesses, while we maintain a degree of emotional detachment or objectivity.

Think about it. Many of the people in a business are there for the long haul. They have contributed to building what exists and perceive that their future depends on it. Like a prized personal possession, the business is something that they collectively cherish and want to nurture. Nobody is more familiar with how the business works or can operate it better.

On the other hand, SVE people typically move around in the organization. They may have a reasonably good understanding of a particular business as a result of working there, but they do not know the business nearly as well as the businesspeople or belong to it in the same sense. SVE people want to contribute to the businesses if they can, but tend to be more open to the possibility that changes are needed or that the funds at the company's disposal could be better utilized elsewhere.

This is not to say that SVE can or should revert to its traditional mindset and behaviors. By creating some new roles, rather than continuing to live out the old ones, SVE can greatly enhance its partnering relationship with the businesses. Table 7–1 illustrates this.

CEO: So SVE people want to be part of the business team while maintaining their independence?

CFO: With everyone operating in the partnering mode, we should be able to strike the right balance. The key is to maintain a constructive dialogue, and work together.

CEO: Do you have some joint undertakings in mind?

CFO: Yes. To begin with, it seems pretty clear that NPV should be the focus for the company's budgeting and strategic planning. I'd like to validate the idea with the businesses and solicit their help in implementing it.

CEO: Some of the businesspeople have a lot of savvy about financial matters, and probably they're the ones you're planning to consult. What about the others, however, who don't really understand the difference between earnings and cash flow?

CFO: We can run seminars, write handbooks, or provide help one-on-one, but I don't believe there will be as much need for hand-holding as you think. Cash flow is far easier to understand than earnings, and there shouldn't be many questions once the budget process is switched over.

Anyone who has ever balanced a checkbook understands cash flow. There is a starting balance, cash comes in, and checks are issued to make payments for one thing or another. Write checks in excess of your balance, and the bank will refuse to pay. As Charles Dickens put it in 1850:

> *Annual income twenty pounds, annual expenditure nineteen nineteen six, result happiness. Annual income twenty pounds, annual expenditure twenty pounds ought and six, result misery.*

Table 7-1. New Roles for SVE.

Old Finance	New SVE
Critic	Ally
Naysayer	Realist
Corporate ("doom and gloom")	Guide

Earnings, on the other hand, have all sorts of quirks. Certain cash outlays are capitalized and depreciated or amortized, generating noncash expenses in the future while other outlays that also create future value are expensed. Various expenses are accrued even though they are not due yet. Most cash receipts are booked in advance, but some are deferred and amortized.

To further complicate things, a variety of accounting and reporting approaches are employed. Many companies wind up with different earnings for internal reporting than for published financial statements, or tax returns, even though the numbers are, of course, reconcilable. Also, you cannot intelligently compare financial data for different companies unless you know what accounting methods they are using, e.g., LIFO, FIFO, or average cost for inventories, expensing or capitalizing software development costs, or using accelerated or straight line depreciation rates.

At first blush, it would seem that there could not be any problem when it comes to income taxes or refunds, because they affect earnings and cash in the same amount. (Other receipts and disbursements have tax effects.) Thanks to deferred tax accounting, however, book income tax expense may differ substantially from actual income tax payments.

Because earnings have been reported with great fanfare since time immemorial, businesspeople accept them as the "bottom line." That does not mean everyone understands exactly what makes up the earnings numbers, but there is a general willingness to presume that SVE knows what it is doing.

Now suppose corporate management announces one day that they're going to run the company based on cash flow. Inevitably, the announcement will be greeted with skepticism.

> Example: A divisional manager at one major European multinational recently commented as follows: "The CFO is really hooked on this shareholder value thing. Out here in operations, where it counts, it means nothing. It simply hasn't been translated into terms that we relate to. We haven't got a clue how to put it into practice."[3]

Shifting the strategic planning and budgeting process to emphasize cash flow will demonstrate that corporate management means what it is saying, especially if the change is also reflected in the company's compensation system. Once that realization sinks in, there should not be any significant problems.

> Example: At one time, Nortel Network's bonus awards were calculated based on an equal weighting of orders, sales, and earnings. As a result, the business managers had little incentive to minimize terms of sale or otherwise control working capital levels.
>
> The CFO lobbied for a change in this formula for several years, pointing out that it really reflected only one dimension of business performance; there can be no sales without orders, nor earnings without sales. His mantra that "cash is cash" became well known in the company.
>
> Eventually the CEO and board agreed, and the bonus plan was changed so that awards would be based on an equal weighting of earnings and cash flow. In the year fol-

lowing this change, Nortel's cash flow results went from chronically negative to strongly positive.

CEO: I hope you're right about everyone focusing on cash flow, because that perspective is sorely needed around here. What's next?

CFO: There is much dissatisfaction with the scorecard for tracking business performance, and justifiably so. We need performance measures that are both soundly conceived and widely accepted, including more nonfinancial measures, and SVE doesn't have all the answers by any means.

Everyone seems to offer the same ideas about upgrading a company's scorecard. The new performance measures need to be comprehensive, forward-looking, and meaningful to people engaged in business activities throughout the company. The scorecard should be balanced, including both financial and nonfinancial measures. Last but not least, the total number of performance measures should be reduced.

Although counterintuitive to some SVE people, who have been trained to think of the results of businesses in financial terms, the inclusion of nonfinancial measures in the scorecard is crucial. The results of customer and employee satisfaction surveys may seem like "soft numbers," for instance, but can provide an early warning of problems that need to be addressed.

Other leading indicators might include new product, service, or process milestones, the percentage of sales attributable to new products or services (for the last X years), product or service quality measures, and cycle times for various activities. Not only are such measures informative, but their inclusion on the scorecard will promote buy-in by demonstrating the value placed on meeting stakeholder needs and fostering creativity.

Say that a company's ultimate financial performance measure is NPV, which is periodically assessed by comparing the estimated value of the future cash flows of each business to the economic value realizable through current disposition. NPV is both comprehensive and forward-looking, but it is clearly not sufficient.

Numerous other performance measures are proposed, and at some point the number of proposals becomes excessive. Here is a thumbnail description of the dynamics at work:

1. The assessment of performance cannot be based entirely on future expectations. Somewhere there has to be a point where "the rubber meets the road," as the saying goes, and actual results are compared to expectations. Otherwise, there would be no accountability for results.

The thrust of an NPV analysis used for strategic planning and budgeting is to assess the present value of *future* results, so other performance measures are needed to track *actual* results.

Cash flow is the acid test of business performance in the long run, but is not necessarily informative over shorter periods. Thus, a business with negative cash flow in a given month or quarter may nevertheless be increasing shareholder value. Surely investors did not expect Wal-Mart to have positive cash flow in the early years, when it was opening up new stores right and left.

It is a good sign for a business to be generating earnings. (Dynamic young businesses generally become profitable well before their cash flow turns positive.) Without considering the capital tied up in a business, however, there is no way to tell whether the earnings are adequate.

Many companies track ROI, which can be calculated on either gross or net asset values (see Chapter 3). An alternative to ROI is *economic value added* (EVA),[4] or operating profit minus a capital charge (e.g., net book assets × cost of capital). Neither of these measures truly indicates whether a business is covering its cost of capital, because book asset value (gross or net) does not equate with economic value.

To avoid the drawbacks of an ROI or EVA approach, the period performance of a business can be monitored by tracking cash flow and earnings against the amounts forecasted in the previously approved NPV projection. If the business is not performing as planned, this will quickly become apparent and the reasons for variation can then be reviewed.

Business team members should have no difficulty relating to the cash flow and earnings versus budget perspective. After all, they committed to these results and have the ability to control or influence the components thereof.

2. Employees naturally want to be part of a winning operation, and also anticipate practical consequences depending on whether the overall results are considered good or bad. Accordingly, they are interested in whatever overall measure of performance the company's management and shareholders are believed to care about, whether it is NPV or earnings per share.

The ability of individual employees to influence the overall results is limited, however, particularly in large companies. For this reason, employees also look for performance measures on the scorecard that are more directly associated with the business activities in their work groups.

Marketing is not accountable for cash flow or earnings, for instance, but it generates sales and expects to see them on the scorecard. Manufacturing makes products, service groups provide services, research develops new technology, and so on. To give the people in these groups something they can specifically relate to, additional measures must be added to the scorecard, e.g., units produced, billable hours, milestones achieved, and patents applied for.

3. Excessive emphasis on output measures can encourage counterproductive actions. For example, marketing might grant longer sales terms as a means to induce key customers to accelerate their orders and carry excess stocks, thereby meeting the sales budget by borrowing sales from future periods (postponing the day of reckoning). In so doing, cash receipts would remain unchanged, exposure to credit losses would be increased, and income tax payments would be accelerated.

To put matters in perspective, outputs must be related to inputs. Rather than simply reporting the number of units produced, for instance, the scorecard might show cost per unit, number of units produced per employee, number of units produced per hour, rejection rate for units produced, and days' supply of inventory.

4. In many instances, financial ratios are more revealing than the underlying numbers. Reporting sales and selling expense as absolute numbers, for instance, will not highlight the fact that selling expense represents a steadily rising percentage of sales.

Financial trends tend to be obscured by short-term fluctuations. Perhaps some of the measures on the scorecard should be shown over a longer timeframe, e.g., a selling expense as a percentage of sales trend line could be reported for the past five years.

Although some people like to review numbers, others relate better to a graphical presentation (bars, trend lines, pie charts, etc.). Charting some of the data, rather than reporting numbers only, may help achieve acceptance of the scorecard from everyone.

5. It is beginning to look as if there will be far more performance measures when the scorecard review is over than when it started, and that is a problem. The human mind can absorb just so much information. Putting too many performance measures on the scorecard will tend to obscure the significance of the ones that the company and businesses really want to drive.

The solution is to prioritize the measures that are in use or have been proposed, and eliminate many of them in arriving at the company and business scorecards for general use. There should be some measures that are common to all businesses; additional measures can be reflected on the scorecards as deemed necessary or helpful by work groups for their respective operations.

Designing the new scorecard is a balancing act; there are no perfect answers, and it is going to be very hard to please everyone. To upgrade the present scorecard significantly, SVE and the businesses will have to pool their expertise and work together. To get started, see the list of performance measures for an "ideal" scorecard in Appendix D.

It should be noted that the scorecard does not meet all of the needs for financial information within the organization. The internal financial statements and associated analyses provide a more complete financial picture of the company and its businesses. The purpose of these reports is to help the businesses make better decisions, so corporate accounting should periodically solicit input from the users as to how the reports should be designed, the appropriate level of detail, and whether other reports are needed.

CEO: I'm not sure what the answers are, but developing a new scorecard is a very worthwhile project. What else is on your list?

CFO: A related study would be whether we should adopt "open-book management," and whether the advantages of sharing the detailed financial results of the businesses with employees outweigh the disadvantages of making this information more readily available to competitors, unions, and external critics.

CEO: Would the business teams have access to corporate financial data and the financial data of the other businesses?

CFO: Yes, and the scorecard is widely circulated. Basically the issue is whether we should put the corporate financial database on everyone's computer.

Open-book management (OBM) is a philosophy that some companies have used to good effect. Although sharing financial information with the entire organization is a key element, OBM also involves providing training to help employees become more business literate, empowering employees to use the information in their work (trusting them as partners), and rewarding employees when the company is successful. If one or more of these elements is missing, the benefits of OBM will not be attained.[5]

While it would be hard to argue with the basic tenets of OBM, the details remain open to discussion. It is not essential, nor even necessarily desirable, that all financial data be made available to everyone in the organization. Giving employees access to a well-designed scorecard, with a balance of overall and unit results, will be a considerable advance over the situation in many organizations.

Also, how much effort should be invested in trying to turn

rank and file employees into financial experts? Here's one well-reasoned vote for a limited approach:

> *What's surprising is the number of companies that adopt the shareholder value mandate but persist in holding training classes to explain value equations to operational people. It is a waste of time. Concentrate, instead, on translating shareholder value into metrics that make sense to the individual's work.*[6]

Still there is an appetite to learn about the financial concepts that the company leadership has embraced. In lieu of formal training courses on shareholder value concepts, which are time-consuming and expensive, consideration might be given to developing a manual, self-instruction course, or videotape that can be shared with whoever happens to be interested. The response may surprise you.

Example: DuPont prepared a Financial Measures Handbook to explain the cost of capital, discounted cash flow measures, and other financial concepts. Thousands of copies of the handbook were sent to various locations in the company over a period of years, in response to "grassroots" demand. Although the benefits of this initiative were not measurable, they presumably exceeded the costs by a wide margin.

Providing incentives for excellent financial performance is also critical. Suggestions along these lines will be presented shortly.

In summary, there is much to be said for OBM, particularly in companies where access to financial information has heretofore been highly restrictive, but OBM is no panacea. The same benefits may be obtainable under some different rubric.

CFO: The next item is "activity-based management," which entails completely redesigning the cost systems of the company to incorporate activity-based costing principles, instead of using "activity-based costing" as an analytical tool. With indirect costs representing an ever-increasing percentage of total costs, the ABM concept has great potential. On the other hand, the training and system conversion costs would be substantial, and it will never be possible to completely model the factors that link activities to revenue streams.

SVE could sponsor an in-house activity-based management seminar, which among other things would focus on deficiencies of the existing cost systems. If one of the businesses emerges as a good activity-based management candidate, we'll scope out a proposal with them.

CEO: Schedule the seminar by all means, and I'd like to be there. Then let's talk some more about this idea.

CFO: The next subject is the advantage of viewing certain business decisions as options. The concept is particularly useful for a dynamic, fast-changing business.

CEO: I guess this really is going to be a learning company. Tell me more.

CFO: The idea is to break big business decisions down into a series of smaller decisions, making it possible to try more things that may fail but have upside potential.

The subject of risk was discussed in Chapter 4. In summary, it is not rational to take an avoidable risk unless there is a potential payoff and the risk-reward relationship appears favorable.

Risk and uncertainty must be factored into business decisions in one way or another, and the process will work better if these factors are acknowledged explicitly. However, many people tend to communicate about risk and uncertainty in a roundabout way, using expressions such as "beyond a reasonable doubt," "a high probability," "a good chance," and "quite likely," that can and do mean different things to different people.

Before an important decision is made, the analyst's assessment of probability should at least be clearly expressed, e.g., "Mr. President, the probability of success for the Bay of Pigs operation is estimated to be about 30 percent. I recommend that _____."

People like to think they are knowledgeable about things, even if they are not, and typically underestimate their degree of uncertainty concerning things that they do not know—whether or not the subject matter falls in their area of expertise.

Example: A methodology called *Decision and Risk Analysis* (D&RA) was introduced at DuPont some years ago by consultant Kenneth Oppenheimer, with Finance and Corporate Plan's sponsorship. The D&RA seminars were well received, and many of the business teams followed up by applying D&RA to real-world problems.

In one of the seminar exercises, participants were asked to respond to a series of trivia questions (e.g., what is the altitude of the highest point in Texas?), with ranges that they considered to have a 50 percent probability of being right. It was a rare person whose ranges were broad enough to encompass 50 percent of the correct answers.

Reasoning backwards from the decision criteria to identify the variables that will influence the outcome, without initially performing any calculations, is a powerful way to identify uncertainties that need to be evaluated before a decision is made. Rather than coming up with a monolithic view of the outcome of a business decision (e.g., a proposed investment has an IRR of 16 percent), the analyst may well conclude that the foreseeable IRR outcomes range from 22 percent to minus 8 percent. Even if the expected result (mid-point of the range on a probability-weighted basis) is quite attractive, the decision-maker should be alerted to the key uncertainties and the impact they could have.

Some of the benefits of D&RA can be obtained by running several scenarios of an investment proposal with alternative assumptions, e.g., high, expected, and low cases. With such an approach, however, there will be a tendency to work out the expected result in detail and then vary two or three of the key assumptions for the other scenarios. Thus, sales growth might be projected as 8 percent in the high case and 2 percent in the low case versus 5 percent in the expected case, producing high and low results that neatly bracket the expected result. The possibility of a major shortfall would be overlooked, even though it was a foreseeable possibility that could have been identified with the more open-ended D&RA approach.

No matter how careful the analysis of a business decision, the conclusion will invariably depend on the assumptions that are made and the future may unfold quite differently. Perhaps the market will stagnate, rather than grow at 15 percent per year, because someone develops a better technology. Or the market may grow as anticipated, but be dominated by a competitor who figures out how to better market their product online.

Although the ability to act quickly is critical, there is also much to be said for retaining flexibility. Where possible, businesspeople will typically make a series of relatively small decisions rather than staking everything on one throw of the dice. Test marketing is done in a couple of cities to demonstrate and refine the concept, before the national campaign is rolled out. A pilot plant is constructed to evaluate the feasibility of a new process, before a commercial-scale facility is built. Microsoft and other big companies acquire stakes in promising new technologies, e.g., by buying interests in Internet startup companies, and wait to see which one pans out.

Such transactions can be described as acquiring options, meaning the right, but not obligation, to do something. Even though it has a cost that may not be recouped, an option has economic value when acquired because of upside potential that outweighs the cost.

To reflect an options strategy in an NPV analysis, it is necessary to incorporate the decision points and the perceived likelihood of success or failure at each juncture in the analysis. See Appendix E for an illustrative case.

CEO: If what you are doing is studying new financial techniques, why do the business teams need to be involved?

CFO: Meaningful financial evaluations require a clear understanding of the business situation, which the businesspeople know far better than we do.

CEO: How would you like to follow up?

CFO: We'd like to start with a seminar on the options concept, and encourage the business teams to suggest potential applications if they see value in it. I've got a first rate individual in mind, who won't come across as an old Finance person, but rather as a new SVE.

CEO: Sounds worthwhile. What else?

CFO: That's all the joint studies that I've thought of, at least for now.

CEO: Here's another one. I keep hearing about the enormous potential of e-commerce, but none of our businesses are into it yet. Is the company about to get lapped?

CFO: That's certainly something that should be looked at. Even if e-commerce would undercut some existing operations, it's better to cannibalize your own business than let someone do it for you.

As discussed in Chapter 1, e-commerce is not simply a new way to run a catalog sales operation. It offers a way to dramatically increase the efficiency of the marketing of products and services, as a result of being able to communicate directly with customers and suppliers. The flip side is that consumers are offered new choices as to how, when, and where they will make their purchases of goods and services.

To date, e-commerce has made the greatest inroads in the marketing of services—securities trading at the click of a mouse, online banking at any hour of day or night, travel reservations, downloadable computer software, etc. For companies in service businesses, there is probably little alternative to going online and the sooner the better.

As for the marketing of physical goods, customers have thus far tended to obtain price and product information on the Internet, but made their purchases through conventional channels. Even if a company is not planning to plunge into e-commerce just yet, it is only prudent to monitor the Internet regularly for price and product information that may be influencing customer decisions.

One of the open questions about e-commerce is whether it will, on balance, result in lower or higher prices. Consumers will have access to more information about available prices, and there are real cost savings that can be shared.

Example: In Europe, e-commerce is threatening national laws and customs that permit retail price maintenance. Thus, a book purchaser in Berlin may find it advantageous to order books from the Amazon.com Web site in the United Kingdom rather than Amazon's Web site in Germany. Even factoring in shipping costs, the price of books ordered from the United Kingdom is much lower because Germany (and several other European countries) permits groups of book publishers to legally dictate retail prices to booksellers.[7]

On the other hand, e-commerce may assist businesses in marketing upgrades and extras, or simply charging higher prices to customers more concerned about convenience than price. Some hotels have found, for instance, that the average price for rooms booked online is higher than for rooms booked via the telephone. Think how nicely a well-designed Web site can display pictures of the higher-priced rooms, a map of how to find the hotel, or a description of area attractions, as well as inquire about the potential guest's interest in having a bottle of champagne on ice.

Although the offering of goods and services on the Internet seems most apparent at the retail level, the impact of e-commerce on business-to-business (or "B2B") transactions may prove even more profound. Business transactions are typically larger in dollar terms than individual retail transactions, and it is imperative for the parties concerned to arrange such transactions as advantageously and efficiently as possible. A technology that permits suppliers to offer their goods and services to other businesses anywhere, while helping purchasers to find the best offers, can hardly be overlooked.

Several e-commerce applications in the automotive (putting the supply chain on the Internet) and computer industries ("build-to-order" systems) were outlined in Chapter One. Similar initiatives are underway in other industries.

Another B2B application is the creation of electronic marketplaces for specific goods or services. For instance, the DuPont Company and others have invested in a Web site for the online trading of bulk commodity chemicals, plastics, and fuel products. Similar ventures are being organized for the matching of buyers and sellers of oil and gas products and services. According to International Data Corp., a Framingham, Massachusetts, market research firm, such activity, in total, will represent more than a trillion dollar industry by 2003.[8]

When planning an e-commerce venture that represents a big departure from a company's existing operations, it may be well to provide for a considerable degree of separation for the new venture rather than inviting an internal battle between the established businesses and new venture.

> Example: When Procter & Gamble decided to undertake an online business of selling cosmetics and hair products geared to the individual looks and preferences of women shoppers, it opted to team up with Institutional Venture Partners (an investment firm in Menlo Park, California) and locate the venture in Silicon Valley. Employees being assigned to the new venture were required to resign from the parent company.

CEO: What kind of e-commerce follow-up would you propose, another seminar?

CFO: If there is going to be a seminar, the businesspeople should probably take the lead, but we may be able to obtain some useful insights from the financial community. As I recall, several of the securities analysts have been asking about our e-commerce strategy.

CEO: What would securities analysts know about e-commerce?

CFO: Very little from a nuts and bolts standpoint, but they probably have been talking to all sorts of people about the financial implications for companies of e-commerce. An exchange of ideas about the potential effect of an e-commerce venture on our stock price could prove invaluable.

Suppose that a securities analyst is assigned to cover an industry. In addition to boning up on information in the public domain, the analyst will doubtless contact the industry leaders, some of their customers, and some of their suppliers in an effort to obtain insights on what the future holds. Information disclosed will influence the analyst's ideas. A securities analyst or investment banker is not likely to say that Competitor A is about to venture into e-commerce, but there might be a revealing question, such as: "Do you agree that firms in the industry could cut their selling and distribution costs by 60 percent with online sales?"

Another perspective that external contacts might be able to offer is creative deal-making ideas, e.g., e-commerce alliances between companies with complementary interests. Merck and CVS recently agreed, for instance, that CVS will sell over-the-counter products on a Web site operated by Merck-Medco Managed Care, while Merck-Medco allows its members to order prescriptions on the CVS Web site.

CEO: Keep me posted about any e-commerce activities of our competitors or opportunities for us. Now, what about incentives for PFP?

CFO: To get everybody on board with PFP, the company should offer tangible rewards for increasing shareholder value. In addition, we need to capitalize on the power of praise and recognition.

"What gets measured gets done," it is said, but this is only true if compensation rewards performance. Employees will quickly figure out how the incentive compensation system really works, so it must be designed with care to ensure that the results will truly be productive.

There is nothing wrong with business leaders getting rich as a reward for rallying the employees at a company and leading them to new heights. Why shouldn't Lou Gerstner at IBM or Jack Welch at General Electric earn as much as top entertainers and sports heroes?

Far more troubling are the cases in which corporate executives have received rich payoffs for mediocre performance. To minimize this possibility, a company's incentive compensation plan should be designed in such a manner that the payoff will be for the long-term creation of shareholder value.

For a public company, the ultimate test of shareholder value creation is a rising stock price. Although a company's stock price is not necessarily "right" at any given point in time, it is a readily verifiable indicator of how things are going for the shareholders. Private companies can use a surrogate valuation approach based on the discounted value of future cash flows, perhaps having an outside firm perform the analysis in an attempt to ensure the objectivity of the results.

Given the availability of stock price information, a long-term stock option plan is a good way to link rewards to superior performance. (Another approach is the issuance of performance shares, which pay off if specified performance targets are met *and* the stock price increases.) This is hardly a new idea, but the stock option plan for tomorrow should differ from most existing plans in one important respect:

➤ Conventional stock options can be profitably exercised if there is *any* increase in the stock price. Such an increase does not necessarily signify good performance, because the stock price can be expected to increase during a five to ten year exercise period unless the company or stock market does very poorly.

➤ Accordingly, the exercise price for stock options could be escalated by say 5 percent per year (which works out to a 63 percent increase in the stock price over ten years) to minimize the possibility of an unwarranted payoff. In such circumstances, more options could be issued in total to ensure an appropriate reward for superior performance.

Of course, the CEO and other top executives are not the only ones whose efforts deserve recognition. Many others may deserve stock options as well, possibly every employee in the company. As with senior management, index the exercise price so that recipients will be appropriately challenged.

There is much more that could be said about compensation arrangements. In addition to granting stock options as an incentive for long-term performance, many companies pay incentive compensation that is geared to achievement of annual objectives. There are also a variety of base compensation approaches, e.g., some companies pay a fixed salary to salespeople while other companies pay sales commissions, and some do both.

A discussion of such alternatives is beyond the scope of this book, but bear in mind the "keep it simple" principle. In addition, the widening gap between the compensation packages of top executives and the rank and file is not clearly consistent with the view that companies are becoming less hierarchical, pushing responsibility down to the working level, etc.

In the long run, such a pay gap could help to undermine public support for the business community. Such support already seems surprisingly thin at times.

Another issue is whether financial rewards are really effective in motivating employees once they have achieved a comfortable level of income. Some writers contend that alignment with the organization's objectives, recognition from management and peers, and a sense of belonging can be equally strong motivators. Such needs are certainly important to most employees, and they can be satisfied without much cost to the company.

Mechanical "plaudits" are ineffective, but a sincere and merited compliment from a boss or colleague can be very, very powerful. Any organization that wants to encourage PFP should create a culture in which such interactions occur frequently.

Picture the annual Academy Awards ceremony. The trophies that are handed out to the "Oscar" winners are not extravagantly expensive, but the recipients will cherish them all the same. The real point is not the trophy, but the memory of walking up to the podium in a room full of applauding colleagues and publicly acknowledging other people without whose help and support the achievement would never have happened. If such a formula plays in "Tinseltown," it should work anywhere.

Example: Emulating a program that the Nortel Network's CEO had established at the corporate level, the CFO instituted annual awards (a plaque and cash gift) for superior contributions by Finance personnel. The program was designed to reward a variety of team and individual achievements, thereby underscoring that anyone who puts their mind to it could contribute to the success of the company.

In the inaugural year for Finance, there were seventy-nine nominations from around the world for the Customer Service Award, the Quality Award, the Teamwork Award, the Innovation Award, the Staff Support Award, the People Development Award, the Manager of the Year Award, and the Spirit of Nortel Award. The motivational impact throughout Finance was tremendous.

There are many other low-cost ways to show appreciation for employee efforts, from donuts (or muffins) at early morning staff meetings to employee of the month awards where the winner gets to take their spouse out for dinner. All it takes to design such incentives is a genuine interest in other people and a little creativity.

CEO: I really like the PFP implementation plan. The concepts of a learning company and partnering dialogue are sound, and you haven't overlooked the importance of putting theory into practice.

CFO: Thank you.

CEO: However, I'd like to discuss accountability.

CFO: Could we get into that next time?

CEO: Sure, see you then.

SUMMING UP

➤ Continuous organizational learning is essential to achieve sustainable competitive advantage, and can be fostered by ongoing dialogue between the businesses and SVE.

➤ SVE can only truly play its proper role by acting as an ally rather than critic, a realist rather than naysayer, and a guide rather than corporate Cassandra.

➤ Knowledge has no value without action, and the new business-SVE partnership must tackle common issues of real substance.

➤ Some joint undertakings will have an internal business and corporate focus, notably upgrading the budget system and performance measurement scorecard. Others will respond to external challenges and opportunities, such as the emergence of e-commerce as a new way of doing business.

➤ Both financial and nonfinancial incentives are essential to make PFP truly effective.

NOTES

1. Joseph H. Boyett and Jimmy T. Boyett, *The Guru Guide: The Best Ideas of the Top Management Thinkers* (New York: John Wiley & Sons, 1998), 84–126. © 1998 Joseph H. Boyett and Jimmy T. Boyett.
2. Paul Hersey and Kenneth H. Blanchard, *The Family Game: A Situational Approach to Effective Parenting* (Reading, Massachusetts: Addison-Wesley Publishing Company, 1978), 168–169.
3. Price Waterhouse Financial & Cost Management Team, *CFO: Architect of the Corporation's Future* (New York: John Wiley & Sons, 1997), 33.
4. EVA™ was developed by Stern Stewart & Co.
5. Thomas L. Barton, William G. Shenkir, and Thomas N. Tyson, *Open-Book Management: Creating an Ownership Culture* (Morristown, New Jersey: Financial Executives Research Foundation, 1998), 3–5. Reprinted with permission from Financial Executives Research Foundation, Inc.
6. Price Waterhouse, op. cit., 59.
7. Neal E. Boudette, "In Europe, Surfing a Web of Red Tape," *Wall Street Journal*, 29 October 1999.
8. Cate T. Corcoran, "Big Brains, Desperate Firms Link Up at Web Site," *Wall Street Journal*, January 20, 2000.

Chapter Eight

THE RESPONSIBILITIES OF PARTNERING FOR PERFORMANCE

Our military forces are one team—in the game to win regardless of who carries the ball. This is no time for "fancy dans" who won't hit the line with all they have on every play, unless they can call the signals. Each player on this team—whether he shines in the spotlight of the backfield or eats dirt in the line—must be an All-American.

General Omar Bradley, 1949

CEO: My question about accountability may have been a bit cryptic, so let me spell it out. PFP is a new mindset and way of behaving for both Finance and the businesses, and it will change many things around here. Change always involves risk, and there will be setbacks as well as successes.

We can't have anarchy in this company, with everyone taking a bow if things go well and blaming others if they don't. When financial problems arise, and they will, who am I supposed to call?

CFO: Call me or one of my people, because financial problems will continue to fall in our core area of responsibility.

Consider the Handy donut that was discussed in Chapter 6. It consists of a solid core of basic tasks and responsibilities, and an expanding area of undefined space that provides flexibility for experimentation, learning, and partnering. In successful organizations, the undefined space in the donut will tend to represent an increasing share of the whole, but the idea is not entirely new and the trend should not be exaggerated.

Even in the "old days," there was recognition that individuals and groups should enjoy increasing autonomy as they got the hang of what they were doing. The point was elaborated on in a situational leadership model developed by Paul Hersey and Kenneth Blanchard in the 1970s, which had four phases: telling, selling, participating, and delegating.[1]

Per the Hersey-Blanchard model, the leadership style should depend on the situation. The initial thrust is to impart basic information, say by telling new employees of company policies and practices. Additional information is presented in the selling phase, but now the emphasis is on explaining why things are done in a certain way and on encouraging employees to act on the information with supervision. The leader steps back as results improve, but continues to participate by providing encouragement. When full proficiency is demonstrated, the leader delegates to the experienced individual or team and moves on to other matters.

Such a progression is neither invariable nor irreversible, for situations will arise that call for a more direct leadership style. Say an experienced team begins to sputter; the leader should probably get more involved by shifting from *delegation* to *participation* (reverting to *telling* would be an overreaction). If people are being asked to do something quite different from what they have previously learned, the cycle may need to start over.

> Example: Jacques Nasser quickly made clear that he was out to shake things up after becoming CEO at Ford Motor. Speaking at an executive training program, Nasser reminded attendees that the auto business is brutally competitive. If meeting the challenge does not make "the hair stand up on the back of your neck when you talk about

it," he added, "then go somewhere else. Go to our competition. We'd love it."[2]

Even in the most knowledge-based of organizations, no one has a donut consisting entirely of undefined space. (Advising someone that their job is to sit around and think is equivalent to saying their services are no longer required.) All persons or groups should have core responsibilities that they are expected to take care of, and be *held accountable* for doing so.

No matter how comprehensive the job description or team charter may be, there will also be considerable undefined space. People can and should *assume responsibility* for matters beyond the core of their donut, and thereby work with others to make the organization a success. Such is the essence of PFP, which can even take place beyond company boundaries (e.g., with customers and suppliers).

> Example: The CFO of Nortel Networks had the pleasure of receiving, on behalf of its U.S. subsidiary, based in Nashville, Tennessee, the Nation's first joint IRS taxpayer quality improvement initiative award. This award was in recognition of a yearlong project that had led to substantial improvements in communications and information between the two organizations. It was estimated that there had been a 59 percent reduction in the average processing time for tax information requests, as well as a more current examination procedure, a reduced auditing burden for both the IRS and the company, and the establishment of a basis for further joint quality initiatives.
>
> In the words of IRS district director Glen Cagle, "The Northern Telecom-IRS team represents the first time in the Nation, or possibly anywhere, that representatives from a company under audit have worked side by side with the examiners to improve key aspects of the audit process."

CEO: Could I still call you if the person that actually caused the problem wasn't in Finance—or SVE, as you now prefer to be called.

CFO: Absolutely, so long as it's understood that the focus will be on fixing the problem.

The purpose for holding SVE accountable for financial problems is to ensure that the proper expertise and resources are brought to bear on the situation. Perhaps it also will be determined that someone acted improperly, in which case sanctions may be needed, but the prime thrust should be to minimize the damage, identify ways to avoid similar problems in the future, and communicate the lessons learned to the organization.

Playing the blame game can quickly undermine the spirit of partnering. Personal sanctions are inappropriate for problems that no one could reasonably have anticipated and prevented, e.g., the sudden bankruptcy of a major customer or a technological breakthrough by a competitor. Even if someone clearly made a mistake, there should be no sanctions if the mistake was not the result of recklessness or malice.

Say that a non-Finance person (X) used a company computer to hack into the system of a securities broker and ran up big losses by trading derivatives. Finance would be accountable for fixing the problem, but only X should be sanctioned.

CEO: What types of risks do you anticipate with PFP?
CFO: That's hard to say, but we will certainly be rethinking some of the traditional checks and balances.

The implementation of PFP does not imply a migration of all SVE activities to the businesses. For treasury, tax, payrolls, etc., a centralized corporate group may continue to be advantageous. Still, there will be greater openness to moving SVE people and activities around as the situation requires, even if this means changing long-established organizational designs and internal control principles.

In years past, a separation between billing and collections was considered necessary to minimize the risk that one or two employees could falsify the billing records and embezzle from incoming revenues. No doubt this principle was established in reaction to specific instances of fraud. If such a separation was not being maintained in practice, say in a regional office with a small number of employees, auditing would write up the situation as a violation. Now some companies are rethinking the billing and collection dichotomy, and in some cases they are reaching new conclusions.

> Example: The CFO of a major insurance company recently concluded that moving collections personnel to the customer service groups would eliminate a major problem, namely the high cost of resolving queries between Finance and customer services. An information technology solution was developed to replace the separation of function safeguard. The new system provided effective controls for matrix-managed groups, e.g., user actions would be recorded automatically and permission to make adjustments withheld pending proper authorization.
>
> The plan was implemented with Finance's sponsorship and the enthusiastic support of customer service personnel, and it achieved service, speed, and quality gains as well as cost benefits.[3]

CEO: There will be many changes in our future organizational structure, or "new company" as I like to call it. The internal and external ramifications will have to be assessed carefully, and, to be honest, I just don't have time to sort things out.

Do you think SVE could play a constructive role in this process?

CFO: Feel free to call on SVE as your "secret weapon" for organizational change. Not only will this save management consultant fees, but also, in my opinion, we can do just as good a job if not better. As the old company is being remade into the new company, we'll bring our vision and experience to the table.

Among the changes that can be expected in the new company, and for that matter nonbusiness organizations, is a blurring and erosion of the traditional organizational structure.

In some instances, as illustrated by the previous insurance company case, activities will be moved around internally without regard to functional turf or preconceptions based on past realities. Alternatively, more effective coordination of the activities of existing groups will be achieved—a result that information technology is well suited to facilitate—without outright combinations that could create new problems and inefficiencies.

There will also be a blurring of external boundaries. As companies concentrate on driving their core competencies, they may find it advantageous to contract out operations that other firms can handle more efficiently. "Outsourcing" brings to mind peripheral activities, from janitorial services to running computer systems, but is being applied to many other activities. Two examples follow:

Example: There are no bicycles being manufactured in the United States now that Huffy Corporation has thrown in the towel. The global industry is awash with excess capacity, and U.S. production facilities simply could not compete with contract manufacturers in Asia and Mexico. Huffy continued to handle the design, marketing, and distribution of its bikes.

Example: As a part of cost-cutting efforts following British Petroleum's acquisition of Amoco, financial reporting, accounts payable, and accounting responsibilities for chemical and oil operations in the continental United States will be outsourced to PricewaterhouseCoopers. Some 1,200 employees of BP Amoco will be transferred to the accounting firm. The 10-year deal was valued at $1.1 billion. BP Amoco is also reportedly close to outsourcing much of its global human resources operations to a California start-up, Exult, Inc. The contract would cover payrolls, benefits, and other administrative work.

A process somewhat analogous to outsourcing takes place when a company is seeking to expand into a new business area. The move may require new technology, a new distribution channel, capabilities in new geographic areas, etc. Developing the necessary capabilities is one possibility, another is a strategic acquisition, and a third is a strategic alliance. In many cases, the best approach may be a strategic alliance in which two or more companies work across organizational lines to achieve results that they could not achieve on their own.

The beauty of a strategic alliance is that the participants can work together selectively without losing their respective identities. Thus, A can work with B in one area, with C in another, with D in a third, and so on. Ideally, the result will be to reap available synergy benefits without creating an unwieldy agglomeration of companies with many activities that do not mesh. If circumstances change, a strategic alliance can be renegotiated or dissolved far more easily than operations created through internal expansion or an acquisition.

However, strategic alliances do not always go smoothly. A recent survey of more than 300 executives by Andersen Consulting indicated that some 60 percent of their post-1997 business alliances had either failed or performed below expectation.[4]

The formation of strategic alliances requires insightful evaluation of the pros and cons, skillful negotiation (including acceptable exit terms if the interests of the parties should diverge), and effective execution. In addition to implementing the business logic of the proposal, many other matters are involved, and the businesspeople will need help, with such things as establishing a structure to minimize overhead, defining financial information needs, and ensuring proper tax planning.

> Example: A U.S.-based manufacturing group entered into a marketing and distribution joint venture with a European manufacturer of complementary products. The venture created what is known as a "commissionaire company" in the Netherlands with branches in the applicable European territories. The commissionaire company functions as a sales agent and does not take title to the goods. The partners' existing sales companies make their own sales in each territory, but do so through the local commissionaire.
>
> By providing one outlet for both partners' products,

the commissionaires boosted overall sales. Profit on sales less the applicable commission continued to go to the appropriate sales company. This arrangement avoided the need to establish a number of legal entities and provided certain tax advantages.[5]

"Virtual" organizations are now being discussed in the business literature. They are groups of companies that work together seamlessly and leverage their individual capabilities to achieve outstanding results. (Another definition of a virtual organization is one that contracts out essentially all of its operations and support services and has very few employees.)

Thus, Kenichi Ohmae describes a 21st century company that specializes in product planning and marketing. This company contracts the product design to innovators in Silicon Valley, who in turn subcontract assistance from software developers in India. The product is then assembled in northern China from electronic components purchased in Singapore and shipped to U.S. and European markets via air express. Payment is by credit card, a universal settlement instrument.[6]

SVE probably has the best combination of expertise and resources to coordinate the evaluation, planning, and execution of such structural initiatives. Meanwhile, other groups can remain focused on developing and driving corporate and business strategies.

Of course, SVE is not really a secret weapon, but its potential for taking on this and other shareholder value opportunities could easily be overlooked—especially if there is still a Finance-avoidance culture in place.

CFO: By the way, just what do you mean by the "new company," and what will it be like?

CEO: There's more to it than the blurring of organizational lines. The "new company" is a metaphor for what the future may hold, not a fully formed concept in anyone's head.

Many elements that have already been discussed will be incorporated in the design of the new company, but its final form cannot be clearly perceived and, like the receding horizon, will never be reached.

The new company systematically develops knowledge, which is then applied quickly and decisively. It does not value change for the sake of change, but recognizes that a "stand pat" strategy is a recipe for disaster. It focuses on the risks and opportunities that are being created in a fast-moving and ever-changing business and financial world, and it attempts to turn them to advantage.

In the new company there will be a tighter strategic focus that reflects an awareness of the realities of global competition, fewer organizational layers, and more real authority delegated to working-level groups. Indeed, some seem to envision that the new company will dispense with managers altogether. As John A. Byrne recently suggested:

> *Success will belong to companies that are leaderless— or, to be more precise, companies whose leadership is so widely shared that they resemble beehives, ant colonies, or schools of fish.* [7]

This seems a bit far-fetched. Bees, ants, and fish do not have stakeholders, nor do they need to continually learn how to do new things. Human beings in organizations do. Orchestras have conductors, football teams have coaches, schools have principals, and companies have managers. However, managerial power and prestige will rest on a new foundation.

Many readers will remember the "Hay point" system, in which a manager's importance or "level" was based primarily on the number of employees supervised, dollars of investment controlled, size of budgets, etc. Such an approach is fundamentally inconsistent with the drive to utilize human and financial resources with ever-increasing effectiveness, and will likely fall into disuse.

Example: George Shaheen recently left his position as the head of Andersen Consulting, the world's largest consulting firm with some 65,000 employees, to become CEO of

Webvan Group, Inc., an Internet start-up company with some 400 employees that will offer online grocery and drugstore services. Although Shaheen gave up a multimillion-dollar pay package at Andersen, his equity stake at Webvan may prove far more valuable if the venture goes well.

Managers in the new company will not be valued for the number of their subordinates and other Hay-point criteria, but rather on what they know and accomplish. A premium will be placed on sharing knowledge rather than hoarding it as a source of power, and on working across organizational lines to achieve common objectives rather than fighting over turf.

Last but not least, the new company must adroitly balance the objective of providing value to its customers, employees, and other stakeholders with the imperative of providing an attractive return to its owners through strategies such as PFP.

CEO: Will the implementation of PFP lead to gridlock? Won't it be nearly impossible to get everyone to agree on all matters and thus get anything done?

CFO: There will often be differences of opinion, which no doubt will be vigorously debated. That's healthy, in my view. After a decision has been made, everyone must get "on board" and support its implementation. However, dissenters should not be required to change their opinions.

In theory, the manager of a business could make all the important decisions personally even though others would have to implement them. Better results are likely, however, if the business manager and principal subordinates make decisions as a team. Not only are teams capable of bringing more knowledge and a variety of perspectives to bear on issues, but advance discussion promotes the sort of buy-in that is essential for successful implementation.

Business decisions almost invariably involve tradeoffs between competing objectives. A product design that is cheaper to manufacture may not meet all the needs of customers; overbooking of flights will minimize empty seats, but may result in passengers being "bumped" occasionally; car seat bags save lives overall but pose dangers for young passengers.

If a decision is left to a person who has been schooled in some particular area of expertise, such as marketing, technical, or Finance, there will inevitably be a tendency to focus on certain outcome criteria and overlook others. The result will be decisions that are suboptimal on an overall basis.

The need to evaluate tradeoffs might seem to be a matter of common sense, but there are always some people who would prefer to concentrate on one particular objective and ignore other valid considerations. Several examples of seemingly excessive attempts to sanction or interfere with business decision making were discussed in Chapter 1.

Striking a balance between competing objectives can be particularly difficult in the public sector. Congress has demonstrated a penchant for dealing with one regulatory issue at a time, often using language that is sweepingly broad and poorly understood, and empowering government agencies to single-mindedly see to the details.

> Example: In 1978, the Tennessee Valley Authority (itself a government agency) was stopped from completing the $110 million Tellico dam, which had been started in the 1960s. The problem was the dam's anticipated impact on a type of three-inch fish, one of a hundred-thirty known varieties of "snail darters," that had been determined to be an endangered species by the Secretary of Interior. The U.S. Supreme Court held that it was clear from the legislative history of the Endangered Species Act of 1973 that "Congress intended to halt and reverse the trend toward species extinction—whatever the cost." Congress subsequently solved this particular problem by enacting legislation that authorized completion of the Tellico dam.

In the new company, the partners (a business or task team) will be in a position to consider all the applicable objectives and evaluate a course of action to obtain the best overall result. Some suggestions follow as to how the partnership should operate in practice.

1. Decisions should not be made carelessly without seeking all the truly relevant information and knowledge, but they likewise should not be delayed until every fact that could conceivably affect the outcome has been considered. By that time, someone else would already have exploited the opportunity and the decision would not matter.

2. The team should be big enough to bring a substantial degree of diversity to the decision-making table, but small enough so that everyone will have an opportunity to speak their mind and hear what others are saying without breaking into subgroups.

3. Ideally, decisions should be made by consensus—not compromise—but it is essential that everyone's viewpoint be fully expressed and considered. If too much value is placed on maintaining harmony, the partnership may glide over real concerns and reach conclusions that, as the saying goes, "are simple, neat, and wrong."

4. If differences of opinion remain after the initial discussion, as will frequently be the case, there are many constructive ways to break the deadlock:

➢ *Prioritize.* Say the decision is of no great importance, e.g., what color drapes should be ordered for the conference room. Have a show of hands for the two favorite colors or flip a coin, a decision gets made, and the partners move on.

➢ *Find a "win-win solution."* Perhaps there is some alternative approach that would preserve the advantages of a proposed course of action while minimizing its drawbacks. By forcing the partners to look for it, disagreement may prove the spur for creativity.

➢ *Take an option.* Break the proposal down into steps. Perhaps the first step represents an attractive option, even though the ensuing steps are debatable. Taking an option is different from deferring a decision, because action will follow without missing a beat.

➤ *Sleep on it.* Perhaps the hour is late, and the issue is important. Mulling it over and then regrouping the next day may help to ensure that the decision reached will represent everyone's very best thinking.

➤ *Study it further.* Say the discussion has brought out a clear need for additional information. Despite the desirability of reaching closure, it would probably be best to table the issue until the missing information can be obtained and evaluated.

➤ *Command decision.* Say that a given subject has been discussed thoroughly, and there is still no agreement. At this point, there may be a temptation to compromise, dividing the difference in an essentially arbitrary fashion. This could be a good time for the business leader to step in and resolve the matter one way or the other.

5. Even after a decision has been reached, one or two of the partners may still harbor reservations. They are entitled to their views, and may even be proven right in time, but the time for debate has passed. Everyone needs to get behind the decision, and work together to implement it effectively.

CEO: In the context of making group decisions, will SVE say "no" at times, as Finance used to do?
CFO: Yes, when it's necessary.

By virtue of being involved in making business decisions, SVE will be able to understand what the business is trying to accomplish and provide inputs in a timely manner. A reasoned explanation of the financial deficiencies of a proposal will often lead to agreement that the proposal should be altered or reconsidered.

Previously, Finance objections would not have come up until the proposal had already gone to corporate management or been agreed upon with an outside party. At this point, the business reaction might have been less than constructive,

("You're always second guessing us" or, "It's too late, we already shook hands on the deal").

It is also possible that SVE reservations will be modified or dropped. Perhaps such reservations reflected a misunderstanding of the proposal, as became clear when the matter was discussed. There may also have been a difference of opinion as to a business matter, e.g., whether the useful life of a new technology is more likely to be five or three years. Taking an interest in business issues is one thing, but going to the mat for an issue in someone else's area of expertise is another.

> Example: A Finance manager who had recently been appointed to head one of the business units at DuPont suggested a selling price increase to improve margins, because prices had remained stable for over two years. The marketing manager said that the price increase would not hold because the three principal competitors would not follow. The unit manager said to try it anyway. None of the other producers raised prices, and DuPont's share of the market fell dramatically. The unit manager sheepishly rescinded the price increase three months later.

Then there will be proposals, as has been true in the past, which seem financially irresponsible or ethically dubious. In such cases, SVE should quite properly exercise its "veto" power, and thereby ensure that the matter will be reviewed at a higher level. This is not to say that SVE is the sole custodian of the company's assets or ethics, for it is not. Any other partner on the business team could do the same thing.

CEO: What title would you propose for the SVE members of the business teams, and to whom should they report?

CFO: If everyone else is a manager, I believe the proper title would be SVE Manager, because it is essential that all members of the team, both in fact and perception, be viewed as equal partners. As for the reporting relationship, what about solid line to SVE and dotted line to the business team manager?

CEO: From what I've gathered, a solid line to SVE would be a tough sell.

CFO: OK. SVE needs to select and train the candidates for the SVE Manager assignments, but we can live with a dotted line while they are working in the businesses.

Of all the facets of implementing PFP, the placement of SVE people on the business teams is perhaps the most critical. It is also a sensitive matter, which must be handled with a combination of firmness and tact.

Generally, the businesses will already have some people with financial training, employed as financial analysts or business financial analysts (BFAs). Rather than being involved in developing strategies and making decisions, the BFAs are more likely to be running down after-the-fact explanations for variances in revenue and expense line items from the earnings forecast. Such activity has its place, but does not contribute much to running the business.

The business team members might well question why one of the BFAs should be invited to sit in on their meetings, let alone be asked to express their views. After all, Joe or Mary is a relatively junior employee with limited experience who has never previously made a contribution (of course he or she was not allowed to). If there was ever a major financial problem, someone from corporate SVE could be consulted. "Don't call us," as the saying goes, "we'll call you."

One way for SVE to defuse such objections is to offer some of its very best people to the businesses instead of keeping them in corporate assignments. As a *quid pro quo*, the new people should be given a title that communicates the role they are expected to play.

Typically, the other members of the business team would be the business manager, production manager, marketing manager, e-commerce manager, etc. If the SVE representative is called a business financial analyst, who will give real weight to their opinions? Nobody, so the SVE representative should have a title equivalent to that of other business team members such as "SVE

Manager" (SVEM). In other words, the partners must be equal—both in perception and reality—for PFP to work.

The SVEM title would be supported by the incumbent's expertise, experience, business sense, and access to the entire financial network (inside and outside the company), not necessarily a host of subordinates. If there are also several BFAs in the business, it seems logical to have them report to the SVEM. Employees running the business cost systems or taking care of other financial activities might report to someone else depending on the circumstances.

To be effective, the SVEM must communicate with, and accept direction from, the business manager, the CFO, and members of the corporate SVE team. It should not make any difference whether one line is solid and the other dotted, or vice versa. The SVEMs that were trained and nominated by SVE will remember where they came from, and if giving them a solid line to the business manager will help sell PFP, then SVE should willingly go along.

It should be recognized that some of the SVEMs will never return to corporate SVE. The very best people on the business teams will go on to become business managers and future business leaders, and the SVEMs will definitely be in the running.

CEO: The PFP strategy seems to hang together very well, but I've got one more question. How will you track the progress towards full implementation?

CFO: I've been working on some ideas for that. If we could get together next week, I'll review them with you.

CEO: By all means.

Summing Up

➤ PFP will increase the scope of SVE responsibilities without reducing its area of accountability.

➤ To tap the full potential of PFP, SVE may need to relax internal controls that have traditionally been maintained and search for alternative ways to achieve the same results.

➤ One of the distinguishing characteristics of the "new company" will be a blurring of organizational lines, both internally and externally. SVE can play an invaluable role in facilitating this process.

➤ By virtue of being directly involved in business decision making, SVE should be able to offer advice in a more constructive way. Nevertheless, there may still be cases in which it will be necessary to say "no."

➤ The placement of highly qualified SVE people on the business teams is a sensitive matter, which must be handled with a combination of firmness and tact.

NOTES

1. Paul Hersey and Kenneth H. Blanchard, *Management of Organizational Behavior*, 3rd edition (Englewood Cliffs, New Jersey: Prentice-Hall, 1977).
2. Kathleen Kerwin, "Remaking Ford," *Business Week*, 11 October 1999.
3. Price Waterhouse Financial & Cost Management Team, *CFO: Architect of the Corporation's Future* (New York: John Wiley & Sons, 1977), 255–256.
4. "Troubled Alliances," *Wall Street Journal*, 7 October 1999.
5. Price Waterhouse, *op. cit.*, 163.
6. Kenichi Ohmae, *The Borderless World: Power and Strategy in the Interlinked Economy*, revised edition (New York: HarperBusiness/HarperCollins Publishers, 1999), 69. Copyright © 1991 by McKinsey & Co., Inc. Reprinted by permission of HarperCollins Publishers, Inc.
7. John A. Byrne, "The Global Corporation Becomes the Leaderless Corporation," *Business Week*, 30 August 1999.

Chapter Nine

EVALUATING PARTNERING FOR PERFORMANCE IMPLEMENTATION

It is better to know some of the questions than all of the answers.

James Thurber, date unknown

CEO: As I recall, you were developing some techniques to track our progress towards full implementation of PFP. How did things go?

CFO: I couldn't seem to address PFP without getting into SVE's role as well.

CEO: That's to be expected. The two concepts go together very well.

CFO: Also, the measurement techniques seem to be in the eye of the beholder. Take this diagnostic table, which demonstrates personal characteristics for each employee.

CEO: Let's take a look.

Table 9-1. Personal path to the land of SVE.

Traits	Inhibitor ("Let's not")	Thinker ("Let's discuss it")	Player ("Let's do it")	Leader ("Let's go for it")
Creativity	How big will the loss be?	We should be able to break even.	Let's improve cash flow by 5 percent a year.	This would double our results.
Initiative	It is against policy.	Let's discuss it.	Count me in.	Why don't we?
Partnering	Have we been introduced?	How can you help me?	How can I help you?	Here, let me help you.
Risk management	It might not work; we can't risk it.	The odds are 60/40; what do you think?	That's a risk worth taking.	Let's do _____ to improve the odds.
Vision	Here's last year's memo.	I read _____ in the Wall Street Journal.	E-commerce is growing rapidly.	How will things look in ten years?

CEO: Some SVE people will have trouble pinpointing their current location on the grid, but there shouldn't be much doubt as to where they should be headed. The real issue will be "How do I get over there?"

CFO: Maybe supporting checklists will help. I have developed them to assist SVE people in successfully entering the PFP world, but, as you will see, most of the points are equally applicable to their business partners. Here's the first checklist on creativity.

Creativity Checklist

Goal: To be a player ("Let's improve cash flow by 5 percent per year") or a leader ("This would double our results").

Leadership Perspective: The company or business cannot cover its cost of capital with productivity gains, especially when the global competition is also getting better every year. Breakthrough thinking will be needed, and there are tremendous opportunities in many areas:

☐ Stay current on the business and financial world and on new financial concepts and techniques by reading, attending seminars, etc.

☐ Cultivate and maintain financial contacts, both inside the company and out.

☐ Listen and learn from people in other areas, even if their terminology and thinking are unfamiliar and effort is required to understand what they are saying.

☐ Look for ways to get the best of both worlds when there is a conflict between business and financial objectives.

☐ Look for ingenious variations on traditional concepts and techniques, as well as totally new ideas about financial matters.

☐ Exchange ideas with others, and use their input to improve the ideas.

☐ Never reject an idea simply because it could fail; anything worth doing entails risk.

☐ Balance your work schedule between specific outputs, partnering activities, and thinking time.

☐ Have fun! A pleasant, informal atmosphere will help everyone to get the juices flowing.

CEO: The ideas about creativity make sense, but shouldn't the goal on these checklists be for everyone to become leaders?

CFO: No one can be a leader all the time or in every area, and anyone who tried would be insufferable. In addition to home runs, we need a lot of singles.

Here's the checklist on initiative.

Initiative Checklist

Goal: To be a player ("Count me in.") or a leader ("Why don't we?").

Leadership Perspective: Continuous improvement requires change, which means (a) undertaking new approaches that will work better than what has been done before, (b) improving on that which is being done satisfactorily but can be done better, and (c) discontinuing activities that are no longer needed or effective.

- [ ] Look for financial practices that are outdated, such as traditional cost allocation techniques, and develop better practices.
- [ ] Champion improvements to financial practices that impact the businesses, such as continuous upgrading of the budgeting process and financial scorecard.
- [ ] Assume responsibility for meeting business objectives rather than simply focusing on the bottom line.
- [ ] Suggest improvements, rather than pointing out drawbacks, when someone has a promising idea.
- [ ] Ask what will be discontinued if a new concept or practice is put into effect.
- [ ] Develop a bias for action. Remember that knowledge is useless without action, and that we can learn by doing.
- [ ] Focus on making things happen and not where the credit or blame will go.
- [ ] Keep a log of instances in which SVE said "no" to businesspeople, what the reasons were, and whether a viable alternative was suggested. Reflect on whether any of these interactions could have been better handled.

CEO: There's some food for thought in that initiative checklist, particularly the need for discontinuing old practices when you are implementing new ones. SVE can perform a real service by reminding everyone of that principle. What's next?

CFO: Here's the partnering checklist.

Partnering Checklist

Goal: To be a player ("How can I help you?") or a leader ("Here, let me help you").

Leadership Perspective: The power of financial thinking will not be fully realized unless SVE becomes an equal business partner. Also, there is much that SVE can learn as well as teach.

☐ Always remember the golden rule of partnering: Treat all the partners as you would like them to treat you.

☐ Contribute to the partnership by maintaining and extending your financial knowledge or expertise.

☐ Listen, listen, and listen some more to what others have to say. Demonstrate understanding and support.

☐ Share financial information and perspectives with business partners, rather than simply stating conclusions, and do it in a way that will be helpful rather than embarrassing.

☐ Recognize that the best decisions will generally require a balancing of business and financial considerations, rather than simply being dictated by the bottom line.

☐ Maintain positions when basic principles are at stake, but do not insist on minor points or claim to be infallible.

☐ Be flexible in your thoughts if it becomes evident that there is a better way or if your original thinking was erroneous.

☐ Work for clear-cut decisions versus mushy compromises that may wind up pleasing no one.

☐ Participate in implementing decisions as well as helping to make them.

☐ Seek out additional responsibilities and tasks, particularly if they do not clearly fit in anyone else's area of expertise.

CEO: The partnering checklist is great, but I suppose you realize that it's essentially generic. Change a few words and it could apply to any other activity.

CFO: That's true, but I don't know what else to do. Partnering is partnering, even though people seem to have trouble practicing it.

CEO: Agreed. My point is that a similar checklist could be used in other areas. What's next?

CFO: Here's the risk management checklist.

Risk Management Checklist

Goal: To be a player ("That's a risk worth taking.") or a leader ("Let's do _____ to improve the odds.").

Leadership Perspective: Risk and uncertainty are unavoidable. Focus on whether the risk-reward relationship is in the company's favor.

☐ Evaluate the downside risks before a decision is made and rest comfortably afterwards (but see the next point), rather than resting first and worrying later.

☐ Remember that the world is constantly changing, for which reason the risks associated with established activities and practices must be reassessed periodically.

☐ Break down big decisions into a series of smaller decisions, and evaluate the first step as the purchase of an option versus a commitment to the entire program.

☐ Take prudent steps to minimize risks, e.g., effective financial controls will reduce the risk of fraud.

☐ Ensure that the risks inherent in important decisions are discussed in quantitative terms so that all concerned will have a common understanding of the exposure.

☐ Try to find out why things go wrong, as at times they will, so that steps can be taken to minimize the risk of similar problems in the future.

☐ Get the businesspeople involved in assessing the risks inherent in their decisions, rather than acting as the devil's advocate.

☐ Avoid practices that are likely to encourage the hyping of forecast results used for evaluating business proposals.

☐ Consider hedging risks where coverage is available (buying insurance), but do not hedge risks that could be more economically self-insured.

☐ Be familiar with the potential and practice of "financial engineering," whereby the creative rearrangement of risks between the parties can facilitate striking an advantageous deal.

CEO: We've discussed many of these points about risk management and I agree with them, but why does the subject merit a separate checklist?

CFO: Risk isn't just a technical matter, it's inherent in all business activities. Don't forget the kind of questions that will follow if something serious goes wrong—where were management, the board, and the audit committee?

Also, SVE people are very sensitive about the "risk averse" label, and some might close their eyes to serious risks in a bid for acceptance. I want to make clear that they aren't supposed to do that.

CEO: Any other checklists?

CFO: Yes, one more. It deals with vision.

Vision Checklist

Goal: To be a player ("E-commerce is growing rapidly.") or a leader ("How will things look in ten years?").

Leadership Perspective: In a rapidly changing business and financial environment, the winners will be those who are best prepared to deal with whatever is coming next.

☐ Keep abreast of external developments and try to think ahead.

☐ Understand history, which shows that the world is a nonlinear place in which unexpected events occur (such as wars, the invention of the printing press, the Depression of the 1930s, or the meteor that wiped out the dinosaurs).

☐ Compare market value to the best internal estimates of economic value, and if there is a sharp disparity, consider whether a market correction is likely.

☐ Remember that others are trying to divine the future too, and consider what effect their conclusions could have on what is likely to happen.

☐ Obtain a range of opinions and thoughtfully consider the reasoning on which they are based.

☐ Evaluate periodically whether the business or financial strategy continues to make sense, or whether new thinking is needed.

☐ Consider external developments that could radically change recent and anticipated trends of sales, costs, and investment outlays. (Thus, oil prices doubled in the last twelve months and the market absorbed it, but what would happen to the world economy if this trend continued for a decade?)

CEO: Since there's no way to be sure what will happen in the future, does it make sense to speculate about what might happen?

CFO: I think so. We won't guess right all the time, but at least the company will develop some contingency plans and acquire a few options. As a result, we won't get caught flat-footed when the unexpected happens.

CEO: Good, please work those points into your seminars for the leadership group. Now let me ask you this. After giving your people the foregoing guidance, how will you, as the CFO, ensure that they follow through on it?

CFO: We'll reinforce the guidance with training, performance appraisals, personnel decisions, and compensation.

Simply telling people to change will not work. They will want to know why the change is desired, need help in getting started, and expect to be rewarded for satisfying the new expectations. If all the leadership group does is hold a series of meetings, most of the checklists will wind up in the trash. There may be a bit more impact if the checklists are distributed and discussed at training sessions, because this level of support will be taken as an indication that PFP and SVE initiatives are considered important. Human nature being what it is, however, many people will still not adopt the new mindset and way of behaving.

To help address this problem, the performance appraisal form will be changed to reinforce the new model. Now SVE people will notice that they are being explicitly rated on creativity, initiative, partnering, risk management, and vision. They will further notice that some of the checklists are being worked into the discussion of things they are doing well and opportunities for improvement.

Imagine that one of the business managers is reminding the SVEM about some of the finer points of partnering. "No one questions your financial expertise, but it would make life a lot easier if you explained the reasons for your viewpoints, so that your business partners could understand where you are coming from." If the comment is soundly based, it should definitely have an impact.

The new PFP/SVE thinking should be taken into account when interviewing prospective employees, deciding who will be asked to participate in important SVE initiatives, and nominating SVEMs. Compensation and other incentives (see Chapter 7) also should be used to reward PFP/SVE behavior on an ongoing basis. It will not take long for everyone to notice that the actions being taken are consistent with the words. SVE people will therefore conclude that the leadership is truly serious about PFP/SVE, and real changes will start to take place.

At the end of the day, there may still be a few old Finance people who are not comfortable with the new PFP and SVE way of doing things. Hopefully, they will realize that they no longer fit in the company and decide to pursue other opportunities.

CEO: What about the measurement of PFP and SVE practices as distinguished from individual performance?

CFO: I roughed out a diagnostic matrix of the key indicators of lagging, average, and leading performance in various financial areas, but it didn't seem helpful.

CEO: Why not?

CFO: Such a presentation assumes that all the traditional Finance practices are deficient, and that we now know precisely how things ought to be done. In my opinion, a bit more humility is in order.

Then another approach occurred to me. In instruction manuals for computers, fax machines, VCRs, etc., there are troubleshooting guides. Things unexpectedly go wrong in organizations too, so why not use the same idea? The format of my guidelines simply states the problem and lists possible PFP and SVE actions to solve it, which should be considered by all the SVE and business partners. No doubt, additional responses can be added, and new issues will be identified as we go forward.

CEO: That's an interesting idea. Show me what you have.

ORGANIZATIONAL TROUBLESHOOTING GUIDE

Problem: Complacency, Failure to Recognize Developing Issues

☐ Ensure that everyone in the organization understands the necessity of attracting funding on a continuing basis and what is required to do so. (In other words, a common awareness is required that a business must earn the cost of capital to survive.)

☐ Leverage business strengths, e.g., by entering new geographic markets.

☐ Be willing to try new things, and to redirect resources that are not being productively employed. ("If you always do what you always did, you will always get what you always got," and that's just not good enough!)

☐ Review restructuring approaches (e.g., leveraged recapitalization or spin-offs) that could help in addressing business weaknesses.

Problem: Internal Focus

☐ Cultivate contacts with customers, suppliers, joint venture partners, securities analysts, investment bankers, and independent accountants.

☐ Share knowledge and information obtained from external sources with your partners within the organization.

☐ Upgrade competitive intelligence and value chain studies, e.g., make full use of information on the Internet.

☐ Reach out for new responsibilities, such as SVE coordination of strategic alliances.

Problem: Unclear or Conflicting Financial Objectives

☐ Initiate a process to upgrade the company and business scorecards and try to achieve general buy-in.

☐ Champion focusing on cash flow and longer-term thinking about financial performance (such as NPV/IRR reviews for the businesses).

☐ Discard financial objectives that are manifestly unobtainable.

☐ Align the budgeting process and incentives with the scorecard, so there will be no mixed messages.

Problem: Ineffective Allocation of Resources

☐ Unify the budget process with longer-term cash flow as the focal point, and hold the businesses accountable for achieving their forecasts.

☐ Sponsor better techniques for recognizing and communicating risks and uncertainty, such as Decision & Risk Analysis.

☐ Consider alternative business strategies with different levels of required resources at the budget reviews, rather than simply discussing what level of resources should be provided for the recommended strategy.

☐ Discontinue products, operations, or businesses that are not adding value and have no reasonable chance of doing so.

Problem: Financial Inputs Being Ignored in Decision Making

☐ Reinforce CEO support for SVE involvement.

☐ Ensure that SVE participates in the decision-making process as an equal partner, so that its inputs can be provided in a timely manner.

☐ Support the partnerships with world class services that will meet or exceed expectations.

☐ Strive to understand the perspectives of business partners.

☐ Educate the business team and be open to learning; we can all learn from each other.

☐ Discuss differences in opinions candidly, recognizing that optimal decisions require a balancing of conflicting views and objectives.

☐ Look for and value new approaches and creative alternatives, i.e., "win win" solutions.

Problem: Poor Execution of Business Decisions

☐ Delegate decision making to the lowest practicable level; people have more zeal for carrying out decisions that they helped to make.

☐ Avoid compromise decisions that gloss over issues rather than resolving them; such decisions can be very difficult to implement.

☐ Ensure that decisions are clearly communicated and properly understood.

☐ Support decisions once they are made, and work together to implement them quickly and effectively. This does not mean everyone must agree.

☐ Maintain high ethical standards; otherwise no accomplishment is secure.

Problem: Failure to Use Knowledge Gained in One Area throughout the Organization

☐ Recognize that knowledge is an asset, and treat it accordingly.

☐ Upgrade financial information systems to make information readily accessible (data warehousing).

☐ Share financial information freely (e.g., open-book management).

☐ Publish "best practice" concepts, techniques, and success stories on the organization's computer network.

Problem: Eroding Financial Expertise

☐ Apply nonfinancial concepts such as the learning organization and Handy donut, which underscore the need to nourish and extend core competencies.

☐ Rationalize and streamline "routine" duties to leave more time for training and education.

☐ Make a sustained effort to identify and stay abreast of promising new financial concepts and techniques, such as activity-based costing and options.

☐ Look for practical business situations calling for new or different approaches or skills.

Problem: Poor Service and Low Morale in Financial Services Groups

☐ Renew emphasis on adding value versus simply cutting costs, and develop a continuing dialogue with business partners about how better service can be provided.

☐ Combine or coordinate financial and nonfinancial activities, such as accounts payable and purchasing, which have traditionally been kept separate.

☐ Outsource services that cannot be provided competitively by internal groups, rather than depriving internal groups of resources.

Problem: Inadequate Incentives for Achieving Objectives

☐ Balance the scorecard by including nonfinancial measures and clearly linking the efforts of individual work groups and overall results.

☐ Align incentive compensation with shareholder value by issuing stock options with indexed exercise prices.

☐ Consider success in applying PFP when making personnel decisions.

☐ Make creative use of nonfinancial incentives to recognize outstanding group and individual achievements.

CEO: I like the troubleshooting guide. Once the problems of an organization have been prioritized, which one has to do because there are never enough resources to work on everything, it suggests focused responses.

CFO: So do you agree that we should move ahead?

CEO: One more thing—Please state your case for the PFP and SVE strategies in sixty seconds or less.

CFO: OK, here goes. SVE offers sustainable competitive advantage for businesses around the globe. Likewise, SVE may be of great value to nonprofits and government agencies that face challenges in attracting funding and optimizing performance. For any organization, a failure to embrace SVE could prove life threatening.

The three basic requirements for Finance to assume an SVE role are functional expertise, Partnering for Performance, and a commitment of all concerned to continuous learning and improvement.

There will never come a time when SVE has "arrived," but the point at which businesspeople start seeking out SVE for advice, counsel, and assistance will mark a true beginning.

CEO: I'm convinced that your PFP and SVE initiatives will increase shareholder value, so let's do it. Good luck!

Summing Up

➤ PFP and SVE are distinct concepts, but should be implemented as a package for best results.

➤ It is relatively easy to map the mindset and behaviors that Finance people must adopt to make SVE a reality, but individuals may need help to pinpoint their locations on the personal partnering grids (i.e., objectively assess their own strengths and weaknesses).

➤ The series of checklists provided herein (along with whatever upgrades might be incorporated) should be reinforced by training, discussion, management coaching, personnel decisions, and incentives. Handing them out with a directive to "go do it" will not work.

➤ Not all traditional Finance practices are outmoded and the optimal future state is unknown (if it even exists). To prioritize the PFP and SVE areas to be pursued, begin by identifying the key problems of the organization. The troubleshooting guide illustrates one possible approach.

➤ By implementing the behaviors, practices, and initiatives of PFP with SVE, any organization should be able to realize significant benefits and increase its value.

Chapter Ten

THE TEN COMMANDMENTS OF PARTNERING FOR PERFORMANCE

God helps those who get up early.

Spanish proverb

I   Thou shalt recognize that while the meek may some day inherit the earth, only those organizations that create shareholder value today shall survive long enough to see that day.

II   Thou shalt recognize SVE people as thy fellow business brethren—created by the same God in the same universe— bringing equal bounty to the business decision-making table.

III   Thou shalt recognize that SVE cannot do it alone and that the core businesses, their leaders, their employees, and the

CEO play an essential role in the creation of shareholder value.

IV Thou shalt view risk as an opportunity to explore unde-fined space and create shareholder value with thy partners.

V Thou shalt accept and understand that partnering with SVE does not mean that thou will never be told "no" again.

VI Thou shalt not confuse—or attempt to pass off—reengineering and reinventing with Partnering for Per-formance using SVE. The latter is the only true path to creation of shareholder value.

VII Thou shalt not permit the past narrow beliefs of manage-ment prophets to cloud the vision of what is possible from Partnering for Performance with SVE.

VIII Thou shalt use the tools of Partnering for Performance—the grid, the checklists, and the troubleshooting guide—to assess thy journey and barriers to reaching the promised land of SVE.

IX Thou shalt not forget that Partnering for Performance with SVE is not a one-time event, but a commitment to continu-ally learn, share information, and trust thy fellow business brethren.

X Thou shalt share this book with—or better yet, buy an-other copy for—thy fellow business brethren as an expres-sion of thy commitment to Partnering for Performance

EPILOGUE

Over the past three years, the PFP and SVE initiatives have had a tremendous effect on the company. SVEMs are now valued members of the business teams, the budgeting system has been overhauled, a new scorecard is in use, and everyone is talking and thinking about cash flow.

One of the businesses was divested on favorable terms, and another business made an acquisition that will speed its progress toward going global. There was a major stock purchase program, funded in large part by reductions in working capital. An e-commerce venture is in operation.

Earnings per share have doubled, and the stock price is up by even more. It is not hard to figure out that the company has been covering its cost of capital. The board is delighted, and there has been positive feedback from the shareholders.

In your time as CEO, however, you have learned that the future begins today. The most obvious benefits of the PFP and SVE initiatives have been realized at this point, or so it seems, but the race to create shareholder value will continue relentlessly. A worrisome little question keeps popping into your mind. What can we do for an encore?

In your messages, there is a note from the Human Resources Director concerning "PFP with HR, the key to superior business results." Maybe this could be a new thrust to keep the momentum going. It is certainly worth discussing.

There is also a voice message from the CFO, who seems to have a knack for doing the unexpected.

This company has been a great place to work, and I've enjoyed every minute. I'll miss partnering with you and many others, but the offer to head up PFP/SVE.com was just too good to turn down. You'll understand when we talk about it.

I apologize that my departure is so sudden, but the timing shouldn't be a problem. Either Allison or Michael is fully qualified to take my place, and I doubt the company will miss a beat.

There is a memento of our many talks in the top drawer of your credenza.

The memento turns out to be a copy of this book with a "thought you would enjoy it" inscription by the CFO and a framed scroll of "The Ten Commandments of Partnering for Performance" that will occupy a place of honor on your office wall.

*   *   *

On reflection and in the spirit of continuous improvement, it occurs to you that there should be at least one more commandment:

XI   Thou shalt not procrastinate in applying the messages of this book, as thy competition may have already purchased their own copy.

APPENDIX A:
COST OF CAPITAL

The *cost of capital* is the weighted average cost of equity and debt financing on a prospective basis. Procedures that a company might use to estimate this benchmark are discussed and illustrated below.

The *cost of equity* represents the prospective financial return to the company's shareholders in the form of dividends and stock price appreciation that would equal the return they could expect on alternative investments of comparable risk. A rising stock price is not necessarily associated with outlays by the company, but stock price appreciation must be included in the cost of equity to realistically reflect the overall return that shareholders expect the company to earn on funds retained for reinvestment.

Estimates of the cost of equity are inherently imprecise, but this value should clearly exceed the cost of debt for two reasons:

1. Shareholders assume considerably greater risk than lenders; they have no guarantee of financial return or even recovery of their investment, and they have no claim to the assets of the company in event of liquidation until all liabilities (including repayment of lenders) are satisfied.

2. Interest expense is deductible by the company for tax purposes, whereas the cost of equity is not.

One common approach to estimating the cost of equity is to start with the current yield on long-term U.S. Treasury bonds, which will be assumed to be 6 percent, and add an equity risk premium of 5 to 6 percent. The latter value corresponds to the average spread between common stock returns and Treasury bond yields over the past seventy-five years.

Past relationships between debt and equity yields will not necessarily hold true in the future, and there are differing opinions as to the appropriateness of the current equity risk premium. Thus, James Glassman and Kevin Hassett contend that equities in the aggregate are no more risky than Treasury bonds over the long term. In other words, the equity risk premium should be zero. [1] It would follow that the stock market is currently undervalued by a wide margin, which seems unlikely.

Suppose that the company takes a more conservative view and assumes an overall equity risk premium of 5 percent. Said premium is then multiplied by the company's "beta factor" (measure of stock price volatility relative to the overall market), which is calculated and published by such firms as Standard & Poor's. In this case, assume that the company's beta factor is 1.4, which results in a risk premium of 7 percent. The company's cost of equity is the Treasury bond yield of 6 percent + 7 percent risk premium = 13 percent.

Cost of debt is the after-tax interest rate that a company would expect to pay for new, long-term borrowings. Assume the company can borrow at an after-tax rate of 6 percent, and intends to maintain a debt ratio of about 20 percent (which might be appropriate, say, for a high technology company that needed to retain considerable financial flexibility).

Now the weighted average cost of capital is calculated, as follows:

Cost of equity	13% × 80%	=	10.4%
Cost of debt	6% × 20%	=	1.2%
Cost of capital			11.6%

Bearing in mind that the cost of capital is an estimate that is accurate at best within one or two percentage points, the calculated result is rounded off to 12 percent.

Financial rates are continually fluctuating, but the cost of capital that a company uses for financial valuations should not be changed unless there is a fundamental change in market conditions. Frequent changes in this benchmark tend to be confusing to the organization and are inappropriate given its imprecision.

NOTE

1. James K. Glassman and Kevin A. Hassett, "Dow 36,000," *Atlantic Monthly*, September 1999, 37–58.

APPENDIX B: DISCOUNTED CASH FLOW MEASURES

Net present value (NPV) is the value of realistically forecasted cash outlays and receipts resulting from a business decision when discounted to the present at a company's estimated cost of capital. A positive NPV indicates that the investment will add value and should therefore, all else being equal, be undertaken.

See Table B-1 for an illustrative NPV calculation of a hypothetical investment proposal in which a $200,000 investment will generate after-tax cost savings of $80,000 per year over its economic useful life (five years).

Internal rate of return (IRR) is the rate of return at which a given series of cash flows discounts to zero. Generally speaking, an investment with a return that exceeds the cost of capital should be viewed as attractive. If there are capital constraints, however, the ranking of proposed investments on a return basis may be useful in deciding which of the projects with positive NPV should be undertaken.

IRR can be conveniently calculated using a computer or programmable calculator. The foregoing investment proposal has an IRR of 29 percent, as shown in Table B-2.

Discounted payback (DP) measures the time required for

Table B-1. NPV calculated for an investment proposal.

Year	Forecast Cash Flow*	12% Discount Factors	Present Value* at 12%
0	$(200)	1.00	$(200)
1	80	.89	71
2	80	.80	64
3	80	.71	57
4	80	.64	51
5	80	.57	46
Total			**89**

*Dollars in thousands.

Table B-2. IRR calculated for an investment proposal.

Year	Forecast Cash Flow*	29% Discount Factors	Present Value* @ 29%
0	$(200)	1.00	$(200)
1	80	.78	62
2	80	.60	48
3	80	.47	38
4	80	.36	29
5	80	.28	23
Total			**0**

*Dollars in thousands.

forecast cash flows from a proposed investment, discounted at the cost of capital, to equal the initial cash outflow. The foregoing investment would have a discounted payback of four years, calculated in Table B-3.

DP ignores cash flows after payback and therefore favors investments expected to quickly generate positive cash flows over longer-term investments. Such an emphasis might be particularly appropriate if the long-term outlook was unfavorable for the industry or country in which an investment was proposed.

Table B-3. DP calculated for four years.

Year	Forecast Cash Flow*	12% Discount Factors	Present Value* @ 12%	Cumulative Present Value* @ 12%
0	$(200)	1.00	$(200)	$(200)
1	80	.89	71	(129)
2	80	.80	64	(65)
3	80	.71	57	(8)
4	80	.64	51	+ +

*Dollars in thousands.

APPENDIX C:
CFO AND SVE
PARTNERS

In a rapidly changing and highly competitive business environment, the CFO must maintain excellent relationships with many people, including:

Board of directors
Bond rating agencies
Business managers
Chief executive officer
Commercial bankers
Committees of the board (e.g., audit, finance)
Consultants
Customers
Direct reports and their staffs: Chief accounting officer, tax officer, treasurer, and others
Employees
Government regulators
Independent accountants

Investment bankers
Investment managers
Outside professional organizations
Peers outside the company
Press
Securities analysts
Senior management members
Stockholders
Strategic alliance partners
Suppliers
Third-party negotiators (e.g., acquisitions, divestitures, and outsourcing)

APPENDIX D:
SCORECARD CANDIDATES

There is no "ideal" scorecard, and many different performance measures can be used. A number of measures that might be considered are listed below. Some are financial, while others are nonfinancial.

Except where otherwise indicated, the results should be reported as actual versus budget (plan) for the period and/or year to date. Comparing the results to those of the prior year (or period) is not recommended, as this would add more numbers to the scorecard, and dilute the focus on meeting planned objectives.

➣ Information presented for each performance measure can be shown as absolute numbers, in graphical terms (trend lines, bar charts, pie charts, etc.), or a combination thereof.

Overall

➣ NPV (long-term projection from last budget review)
➣ IRR (long-term projection from last budget review)
➣ ROI (earnings divided by gross book value of assets)
➣ Cash flow
➣ Earnings

Marketing

> Sales (revenues)
> Selling price per unit
> Selling price index (2000 = 100)
> Number of new accounts
> Number of lost accounts
> Average revenues per account
> Customer satisfaction (survey results)
> Estimated global, region, and country market share
> Global, region, and country market rank
> Percent of sales outside the home country
> Percent of sales for new products (last X years)
> Days' sales outstanding
> Bad debt write-offs

Production

> Cost per unit
> Units per hour
> Units per employee
> Yield (inputs/outputs)
> Reject or rework rate
> Days' supply of inventory
> Cycle time (production to shipment)

Services

> Cost per transaction
> Transactions per hour (or other time unit)
> Billable hours per hours worked
> Quality of service (e.g., X percent of customer inquiries satisfactorily resolved on first call from customer)
> Customer satisfaction (survey results)

Technical

> Cycle time (new products)
> New product or process milestones

➤ Patents applied for
➤ Patents issued
➤ Licensing revenues

Materials & Logistics

➤ Purchase price index (2000 = 100)
➤ Number of vendors
➤ Number of vendors for X (a major raw material)
➤ Cycle time (purchase to delivery)

Human Resources

➤ Headcount and number of temporary employees
➤ Headcount (dedicated employees) of contractors for out-sourced activities
➤ Number of outside contractors
➤ Training hours
➤ Employee satisfaction (survey)

All Areas

➤ Variances of more than 10 percent above or below budget (year-to-date)
➤ Special accomplishments (in ten words or less)

APPENDIX E:
OPTIONS

In financial terms, an option is the right, but not obligation, to do something. Examples might include the right to purchase a piece of real estate or to buy ("call") or sell ("put") a given stock, within a specified period of time at a stated price.

An option has value when acquired because it gives the holder a choice that is potentially advantageous (e.g., a call will be exercised if the market price of the stock exceeds the exercise price). It also has a cost, which must be weighed against the potential benefit. Sophisticated mathematical techniques have been developed to value options, and thereby assist market participants in setting the prices at which they should trade.

Many business decisions are of an analogous nature. For example, a research and development program can be viewed as an option to commercialize the technology that may result. Ultimately, the value of such an option is a function of the probability of success and the potential payoff.

To assess such a decision using discounted cash flow techniques, it is essential to incorporate the applicable decision points and perceived likelihood of success or failure at each juncture in the analysis. An illustrative example follows for a three-phase, new product development program. For simplicity, all data are presented on an after-tax basis.

Step A (year 0) involves $500 thousand in research expenditures. There is a 40 percent chance that the technology will be assessed as having commercial potential, and a 60 percent chance that it will not and the program will be terminated.

Step B (year 1) involves $3 million for a program to refine the concept and demonstrate commercial feasibility. It would be undertaken if step A had a successful outcome, with a 50 percent probability of commercial feasibility.

Step C is a full-scale rollout with an outlay of $5 million in the second year, cash flow breakeven in the third year, and positive cash flows in years four through eight (after which the expectation is that the product will be outmoded by the next generation technology).

Is this program viable from an economic standpoint, even though there is only a 20 percent probability (40% × 50%) that the new technology will be commercially successful? Yes, because the anticipated cash flows on a probability-weighted basis (see Table E-1) are attractive.

Using the techniques explained and illustrated in Appendix B, the probability-weighted cash flow can be used to calculate the attractiveness of the program on a discounted cash flow basis. Thus, the program prior to undertaking the research and development offers:

Table E-1. Options analysis.

Step	Year	Cash Flow*	Chance of Doing	Probability-Weighted Cash Flow*
A (R&D)	0	− 500	100%	− 500
B (Demo)	1	− 3,000	40%	− 1,200
C (Full)	2	− 5,000	20%	− 1,000
"	3	0	20%	0
"	4	5,000	20%	1,000
"	5	10,000	20%	2,000
"	6	12,000	20%	2,400
"	7	8,000	20%	1,600
"	8	5,000	20%	1,000

*Dollars in thousands.

➤ NPV—$1,750 thousand
➤ IRR—26 percent
➤ DP—six years

Although obviously imprecise, these results provide a rational basis for deciding to undertake Step A of the program (despite an 80 percent probability that the program will "fail") and a starting point for future evaluations as to whether subsequent steps should be undertaken.

INDEX

IRR, *see* internal rate of return
IRS, *see* Internal Revenue Service
ITT, *see* International Telephone & Tele-
graph
ITT Industries, Inc., 120

Japan, 21
Jefferson, Thomas, on knowledge, 136
Johari Window, 136–137
Johnson & Johnson, 126–127
junk bonds, 26

Karmazin, Mel, 37
"keeping the books," 99
Keynes, John Maynard, on profit, 25
KKR (Kohlberg Kravis Roberts & Co.), 64
knowledge-based economy, 65
Kohlberg Kravis Roberts & Co. (KKR), 64
Kroc, Ray, 8
Kunz, Heidi, 120

L. L. Bean, 8
labels, 115–117
LAFTA, 3
Lao-tzu, on beginning a journey, 135
Latin America, 112
layers, organizational, 45
leadership, 160, 167
"lead steer" investor, 43
learning organizations, 135–136
leveraged recapitalization, 62–63
Levi Strauss, 114
Lewent, Judy, 88
lifecycle costing, 51
"line" people, 115
Long-Term Capital Management LP, 19
Lucent Technologies, 21, 38
Luft, Joe, 136

Machiavelli, Niccolo, on introducing new
things, 131
Malkiel, Burton, on U.S. economy, 21
managers, 167–168
Managing for Results (Peter Drucker), 69
marketing focus, *xvii*, 121
markets, identification of new, 51
matrix-management, 112, 163
McAdams, Lisa Daniels, on respecting oth-
ers, 111
McCaw Cellular, 42–43
McDonald's, 8
MCI, 121
McKinsey & Co., 69
Melloan, George, on incentives in govern-
ment, 44

Merck, 88, 153
Merck-Medco Managed Care, 153
Merrill Lynch, 16, 21
Mexico, 164
Microsoft, 10, 21, 31, 60, 86–87
Milken, Michael, 26
Mobil, 29, 30
monetary policy, 26
money markets, equity markets vs., 25–26
Morgan Stanley Dean Witter, 21
motivators, 155

NAFTA, 3
Nasdaq, 16, 17
NASD (National Association of Securities
Dealers), 16
Nasser, Jacques, 160–161
National Association of Securities Dealers
(NASD), 16
needs assessments, 125
"Need to know" emphasis, 113
negative perceptions of Finance, 115
net present value (NPV), 33, 55–58, 83,
141–142, 149, 201
"new company," 163, 166–168
Newton, Isaac, 129
New York Federal Reserve Bank, 19
New York Stock Exchange (NYSE), 17, 26,
38
nonfinancial measures, 141
nonprofit organizations, 45–46
Nordstrom, 10
Nortel Networks, 7, 37–38, 79, 98, 121,
140–141, 155–156, 161
Northern Telecom, 7
see also Nortel Networks
Northwest Airlines, 4
NPV, *see* net present value
Nucor Corporation, 129
numbers, forms of, 119–120
NYSE, *see* New York Stock Exchange

OBM, *see* open-book management
Ohmae, Kenichi
on achieving perspective, 8
on 21st-century company, 166
open-book management (OBM), 145–146
"operating" people, 115
Oppenheimer, Kenneth, 148
opportunity cost, 124
options, 149, 170–171, 211–213
organizational cultures, *see* corporate culture
organizational layers, 45
organizational structure, 112, 115–116